Forward

This book is dedicated to my amazing parents, Gerald & Beverly Rosenthal. I wouldn't be successful today without their total support, guidance and love.

Also, to my incredible wife Diane, as well as our three children: Jessica, Samantha and James. You put up with all of my animals, both in our sanctuary and in our house!

I would also like to thank Evelyn Larabell, one of the best teachers (and friends) I have ever known, for taking the time to edit these stories.

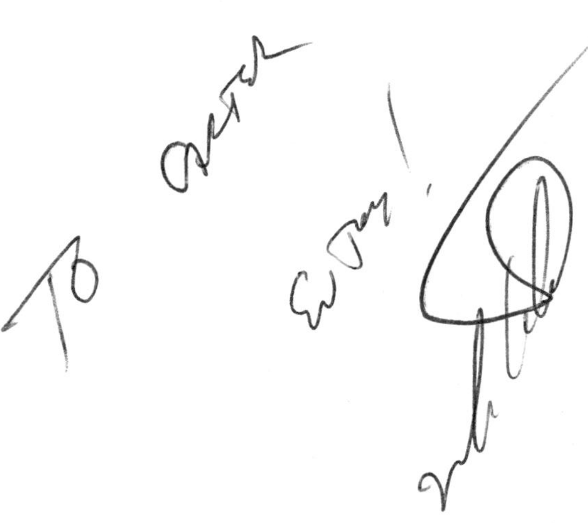

Chapters

Chapters (continued)

Chapter One

Werewolves of London

I obtained a binturong, also called a bear cat, on April 7, 2010 after it had attacked a zookeeper the previous week. Binturongs are the longest prehensile-tailed mammal in the world. Each one of their feet has razor sharp claws that enable them to climb up trees, since they are arboreal. They also have extremely large canines, as well as a full set of teeth. They are quite dangerous but are known in their native Malaysia to be kept as house pets like we keep dogs in our country.

Of the 20 binturongs we've had over the years, only one was a problem. We named him Diablo; he wasn't really that bad. I could go into his cage to clean and feed him, but he didn't want to be petted or be near anyone. Well, this one was vicious from the get-go. I acquired it on Wednesday and the following Friday, it severely mauled me. I think it's safe to say that it's the worst attack I've ever had. When it was all said and done, I had 91 bites and was literally scratched from the very top of my head down to the very bottom of my left foot. One of the fangs (canines) had gone right through the bottom of my shoe into my foot.

Let me back up to the beginning. This animal was extremely vicious… I couldn't even open the cage door to put food or water in without him trying to attack me. It was an escape-proof, large, outdoor, chain-link fence. I used to house an adult lion in it. So what I would do, since he loved marshmallows, is take a big marshmallow and throw it through the fence to the back of the cage. He would run to get the marshmallow! As soon as he turned to run, I would quickly open the door and replace the old food and water dishes with the fresh ones. Well, that worked for about one week until he outwitted me. I threw the marshmallow into the cage, like I had been doing for a week. He turned and took one step toward it. I opened the door to his cage and he pivoted. He never had any intention of going for the marshmallow as he lunged at me!

He pushed his head out of the door just as I was shutting it. His head was on the outside of the cage, the rest of his body was inside the cage, and the door was pinning his neck so he couldn't move forward or backward. I had him trapped. I wasn't choking him, but he couldn't move anywhere. He was spitting, growling and trying to claw his way to attack me but he couldn't. He also couldn't get back into his cage. I was in a dilemma. I had no choice but to open the door. I knew that only two things could happen. The first is that he would retreat back into his cage. The other is that he would come out and attack me.

I opened the door a little bit, hoping he would go back into the cage. He went with option #2. He came at me and sunk his fangs (canines) into my left thigh, narrowly missing my femoral artery. I have two scars to remind me how close I came to dying that day. He then let go and ran the opposite way. I had to make a split-second decision. I could have run into his cage and shut the door behind me, locking me in and him out. This would have saved me but would have left him free to escape and severely injure someone in the neighborhood. In fact, after knowing what he did to me, I'm pretty positive he would have killed someone. There is no adult that would have stood a chance, let alone a child. I was extremely lucky to have survived his attack. I would never have been able to live with myself knowing I was the cause of something that awful, so I went with my other choice, which was to jump on his back and sacrifice myself to try to get him back into his cage. I was fully aware that he might kill me, but I had to try.

I quickly jumped on his back trying to grab him. He turned and started biting and scratching me. Never in a million years did I think it would turn out as badly as it did. He was scratching me throughout the whole fight, but I don't really remember it all. I knew that I had bites and scratches all over my body, because I still have most of the scars to show for it. I wasn't sure how I was going to get him back in his cage, because I didn't have any time to think any of this out in advance. I grabbed his tail, after wrestling on the ground for quite awhile, or so it seemed, and I was sort of swinging him around in a circle to prevent him from attacking me anymore. I was trying to make him dizzy and give myself a second to think about my next step. I decided to keep swinging him while I tried to make my way back near his cage to attempt to throw him back in when I saw that his door had swung closed. It wasn't locked or shut tightly, but it was closed, to the point that I would have to open the door to put him into the cage. That meant that I would have to stop swinging him.

I released his tail for a split second while I swung his cage door open; he turned and started to run the other way. This time I leapt and just caught the end of his tail. It was now time for Round Two. He turned to attack me. He was extremely mad at this point. You have to picture this…I didn't know what else to do. I really thought I was going to die. I was lying on the ground and I couldn't see very well because I had blood all over my face. He hadn't bit the top of my head just yet. That's coming up. I had his tail and there was no way I was going to let go. My legs were fully extended with his tail between them. I had his three-foot tail fully extended while he was biting at my feet. I had tennis shoes on, so I didn't think there was any chance that he would penetrate my shoes. This temporarily gave me about 20-30 seconds (even though it seemed like forever) to try to think about what I was going to do next, while he was still biting at my feet. I wasn't in pain at that point. It didn't work. He ended up biting through my left shoe and sinking one of his fangs into the bottom of my foot. I don't remember letting him go, but I guess the pain was too much. That's when he must have made his decision to finish me off instead of trying to run anymore. He leaped for my neck and I ducked to protect my throat. He sank his fangs into the top of my skull, causing a lot of blood to stream down my face, making it more difficult to see. I grabbed him and somehow got him on the ground. I now thought that he was like a dog or a cat where I could possibly get him behind the head and grab the scruff of his neck. I thought he wouldn't be able to do any more damage with his fangs and that I might have a chance of somehow tossing him in his cage, even though I knew he could still rip me open with his claws.

I was within three feet of his open cage door, when I reached down and went for the scruff of his neck only to realize that binturongs don't have a scruff of the neck! Bad idea. It's funny for me to say now, but it wasn't at the time. It was during that split second that he turned and sank his fangs into my left palm, ripping my hand completely open. My palm was hanging down and my left hand was now useless. The rest is a blur but I know that we were struggling for at least 10-15 minutes, even though it seemed like forever. There was nobody around to help me and yelling wouldn't have done me any good. Lord knows, I tried. There was no way that I was going to let this monster get away; I knew that I had to get him back into his cage.

I remember thinking that I might die now, so I would just take more bites and hopefully survive while I just grabbed him and hung on while running us both into his cage and shutting the door behind us. I realized that I would be locked in the cage with him and I probably wouldn't survive, but better that I got hurt than to have him loose where he could severely injure others. I grabbed him and somehow got extremely lucky by swinging him through the door into his cage. I put the lock back on and remember collapsing to the ground. I know there was blood, all mine, all over the chain link fence and ground. I couldn't really walk because I was bleeding profusely as he just narrowly missed my femoral artery with two of his bites.

My phone was in the sanctuary. I don't remember this, but I must have opened the door and crawled across the floor to where I left it. I only knew this because there was a trail of blood going from the door to my phone. I retrieved my phone and then crawled back outside to the binturong's cage before calling my wife. I guess I wanted to make sure he was still locked in the cage. She was in our house and came outside to find me lying on the ground in a pool of blood. She said that there was blood everywhere and that I repeatedly kept asking her if the binturong was still in the cage. She kept telling me that he was secure. She said that I was hurt so badly that she had to call 911. Of course, me being the tough guy that I am, I told her that there was no need to call 911; I didn't need an ambulance.

I just asked my wife to help me up to the house, because I couldn't walk. I had her bring me a nearby shovel that I could use as a walking stick. I don't remember the long walk to the house. I remember her very clearly telling me not to let our son see me. James was two years old at the time this happened. I really couldn't figure out why she didn't want him to see me. I knew that I was bleeding a lot and that my left hand was just hanging but I figured I could hide that. I was holding it together with my right hand! I just wanted to get to the bathroom and clean up a little to see how badly I was hurt. What I didn't realize was that blood was streaming down my face from the puncture wounds to the top of my head. I was also covered in blood from the bites and scratches to my face. I was in shock and didn't feel them. The only pain I felt at that time was my left hand and my left thigh. My shirt and pants were shredded and covered in blood, as well. I didn't realize how badly I looked until we got in the house and my wife helped me upstairs into our bathroom. I looked in the mirror and I had holes all over my face. One fang narrowly missed my left eye, another was just outside of my right ear and another was just inside my left nostril. Had he jerked his head up with that one, he would have ripped off my nose! I had bites on my neck, and my chest was all scratched up. I had claw marks on my left side, two fang punctures on my left thigh, two deep punctures on my left ankle and a puncture on the bottom of my left foot. All of these are now scars to help me remember that day…like I would ever forget it!

I was covered in bites and scratches and I knew that I had to get to the hospital. I couldn't put my shoes on because of the wounds, the bleeding and the swelling, so I had to go barefoot. I changed into shorts because of the wounds to my left leg. My left hand was wrapped in a towel. It was fairly cold outside and I looked pretty funny going out like this. I looked like death warmed over. I tell everyone at my shows that the staff at St. Joseph Hospital knows me on a first-name-basis because I get hurt so much. My audiences think I'm joking. I'm not! My wife drove me to the hospital and dropped me off at the emergency door while she parked. They wheeled me in and the lady at the desk looked up and asked, "Mark, what happened?" I said that a binturong got me, and while we were talking, remember that this was a very busy Friday night with a packed waiting room, two ER doctors came running up and said, "Mark, come right on back." I guess it helps to be famous, or maybe infamous.

I bypassed the whole crowd and went directly into the back where they said I was lucky to be alive. A few different doctors examined me and then a technician came in to take me to X-Ray, just to make sure nothing was broken. Amazingly, I had no fractures. I was extremely lucky. After my attending doctor consulted a couple of specialists, they all came to the conclusion not to suture any of my wounds because of the probable infection that would occur. It would have nowhere to drain and would infect my whole body. They bandaged me up and told me to have them changed three times a day and to put antibacterial ointment on all my wounds. They prescribed double doses of antibiotics and pain pills and then sent us on our way.

It was after 11 p.m. at this point and I felt awful, not because of the bites and scratches, but because I always take my wife out for our date night on Fridays and now that was ruined. Neither of us had eaten and I told her that I still wanted to take her out. It was way too late for a movie, but we could still go somewhere for dinner. She thought I was crazy to want to go out in my condition, but I really wanted to take her somewhere. Keep in mind that I looked like I was just released from a war. I had bandages on my face, my hands, my legs and my left foot. Oh yeah, I was barefoot and in shorts too! My wife said that there was no restaurant open. I thought that Denny's was, so we decided to go there. I knew they wouldn't serve me without any shoes, but there was no-where open to get any at that time. We passed a Rite Aid Pharmacy where I needed my prescriptions filled, so I had her stop. I was hoping to find a pair of flip flops that I could wear just to get in the restaurant. The lady behind the counter knew me from my shows and asked me what happened. I told her and asked if they had any flip flops that I could purchase. She said that they were all sold out of men's but they had a few women's left. I figured I had no choice, if we wanted to go out, so she showed us where they were. They were sold out of extra large and they only had one large size left. They were pink! They didn't fit and my feet hung over both the front and the back ends. I bought them anyway, filled the prescriptions and off we went to Denny's.

I don't know if you have ever been there late on a Friday night, but it's not really a normal crowd. I limped in, wounded, on pain killers, wearing shorts and women's pink flip flops. I was definitely a sight to see. We sat down, ordered our meals and ate. Not one person questioned why I looked like I did! I couldn't have picked a better time to get attacked, because I had no shows for the next two days. This was a rare weekend that I wasn't booked, so I could rest for the two days following this ordeal. I had shows every day the following week, starting off with four of them on Monday. I drove myself and did all four shows while still heavily bandaged. There is no way that I'm ever going to miss a show and disappoint people.

I lined up a permanent home for the binturong at a zoo in Virginia. Grant, the owner of the zoo, and his helper came to pick Diablo up after my shows on Monday. Grant is very well known and has done quite a few major motion pictures with animals. His most recent was, "Furry Vengeance."

I told Grant on the phone this was the meanest binturong I had ever seen and he said he wasn't worried. He changed his mind within seconds of seeing him! He said there was no way he was entering the cage to crate him. I had to capture this psycho binturong for them to transport because they were too scared to enter his cage! Remember, it had been only two days since the binturong attacked me, and my left hand and arm were still bandaged. I had trouble walking also.

I came up with a plan. Grant was to distract Diablo with marshmallows while I entered his cage with a large travel crate, preloaded with lots of marshmallows and bananas. I would close the door once Diablo was in the crate. OK, that was my plan, but not all plans work out as intended.

Diablo climbed up his ladder near the far corner of his cage to get the marshmallow Grant was holding. I opened the cage door and quickly entered with the carrier. Diablo saw me and came running, forgetting about the marshmallow. I dropped the crate and barely got out of his cage. He was within inches of my back when I closed his door!

I succeeded in placing the crate in his cage, but the door had swung closed when I dropped it. Diablo wanted the food, but couldn't get to it. None of us were about to enter his cage to open the crate door for him. I grabbed a snake hook and put it through his cage bars to try and catch the crate door to swing it open. Diablo kept attacking the snake hook, making it very difficult. I finally hooked onto the door of his crate and swung it open.

Daiblo ran into the crate to eat, and I immediately dropped the snake hook and opened his cage door. I jumped onto the top of his crate and reached over the front to swing his door closed. He came at me but I was faster. I proceeded to close and latch the door, securely trapping him!

Grant called me the following morning and told me that Diablo had already bred with his female when he put them together. End of story. I don't hold it against the binturong because I knew he was mean when I got him. I didn't take the right precautions. It was 100% my fault, not his. Everything turned out for the best for the binturong and me in the end.

Chapter Two

Little Bunny Foo Foo

I've always had a love of animals. I kept many different species of reptiles growing up as a little boy. I had an anole (also known as a common chameleon) and a few little rainbow lizards. I remember when I was 13 years old that I took my moped for about a 10 mile ride. For all you kids out there…that was a little motorized bicycle that I could ride as either a bicycle or use the gas, as it was gas powered.

I was driving along Woodward Avenue in Royal Oak, Michigan when I saw a rabbit in the road that had been hit by a car. It must have been recently hit but was still alive. It was bleeding and obviously injured. I stopped, picked it up and drove around looking for a box to put it in. I found a box in a dumpster and placed the bunny in the box on the back of my moped. I drove it over 10 miles back home.

When my mom got home, I was very distraught over this rabbit. I asked her to do something about it and make it better. I remember my mom putting this bleeding rabbit on our kitchen table, where we ate, on newspaper and calling a veterinarian to see what we could do. The poor rabbit died before she was even done with the phone call. My mom said not to tell my dad about the rabbit on our table. We took the rabbit in our backyard and buried it. That was one of my earliest memories of my compassion toward animals.

Chapter Three

This Snake is Gonna Be the Death of Me!

January 27, 1987 is a date that I will never forget, because it's the day that I actually died…not once, but twice! I graduated from Michigan State University with a Bachelor of Science degree in Biology. I was living in Lansing, Michigan with my roommate named Shay. She had recently moved in with me and my other roommates: a dog, various reptiles and a bunch of other pets. I also had, in my living room, some baby Indian cobras and a three foot long Western Diamondback Rattlesnake. For those of you who don't know much about venomous snakes, the Western Diamondback is the second largest rattlesnake in the world and the most venomous! I had no business having one in my living room, let alone the cobras. I was pretty immature back then and I thought that nothing could ever happen to me. Boy, was I wrong!

I held these snakes with no protection at all…no gloves, snake hooks or snake tongs…just with my bare hands. I would grab them behind their head and proceed to take them out. Well, on this particular day, I had just cleaned the cobra's cage and was in the process of cleaning the Diamondback's cage. I usually held him out in my left hand while I cleaned the cage with my right. My roommate was sitting on the couch watching T.V. and she said something to me. I don't remember what it was, but as I turned to my left to respond to her, I guess my right hand apparently came over near my left and the snake sunk his right fang into the middle finger on my right hand. I immediately felt the venom being injected into my finger. It was an incredibly burning sensation. I remember saying the following to my roommate, “Shay, I’m going to die.” She was very calm, as was I, probably because neither one of us actually thought the worst was about to happen. I found out later that me being calm and relaxed probably saved my life.

I placed the snake back in his cage, after I finished cleaning it! I went into the kitchen, all the time holding my right arm down so as to slow down the venom. I then placed my hand under ice cold water so as to freeze it and slow down the venom. You could clearly see the venom traveling up my arm in the form of a red streak. I knew that if the red streak went all the way to my heart, then I would die. I told Shay that I was going to go upstairs and change my shirt, because I wanted to look good in case I didn’t make it. I know…not too logical thinking, huh? I came back down, after putting on my favorite shirt, and we both noticed that my arm was really starting to swell. I was going to drive myself the 20 minutes it took to get to Sparrow Hospital in Lansing. Shay said no, that she would take me.

I barely remember that drive. I clearly remember the burning going up my arm…it was exactly as I had read. It started in the finger where I was bitten, and proceeded to radiate up my arm…extreme intense burning pain, like a red hot poker traveling up my arm.

I told Shay to go as fast as she could. I needed her to speed. I figured we would get a police escort had we been pulled over, because this was a matter of life and death. As luck would have it there were no police officers, and we went over 100 miles per hour the whole way there.

I want to point out that I hadn't lost consciousness yet. She got me to the hospital in record time and from this point on, I don't remember too much. I know I went into emergency and told them what had happened. They yelled for help and I was immediately seen by a doctor while everybody else rushed around behind him. I remember them cutting off my shirt, which I wasn't real happy about, because it was my favorite one. They had to cut it off because my arm had swollen so much by this point that they couldn't remove my shirt the normal way. That's about all I really remember until waking up the next day after surgery.

I was told that they had to operate on me and that I actually died twice while on the operating table. They obviously brought me back both times, eleven vials of anti-venom had to be flown in by helicopter for me. What made matters worse was that I was allergic to the anti-venom since it's acquired from horses and I am highly allergic to them. The doctors told me that I would have died from the venom anyway, so they had to administer the anti-venom. I ended up suffering from serum sickness, which is a severe allergic reaction to the anti-venom. Keep in mind that only one of his fangs penetrated my finger…about 1/8 of one drop got into my system; that's it! Had both fangs penetrated my finger, then I would never have even made it to the hospital. I developed something called serum sickness after receiving the anti-venom. I am highly allergic to horses, and back then, the anti-venom was also called horse serum. It was derived from horses. I developed a very high fever (above 105 degrees F) while in the hospital and black spots all over my body that itched very badly.

Needless to say, I wouldn't wish this sickness on anyone. The surgeons said that my finger and hand were pretty bad and that there was a chance they would have to amputate my right arm at the shoulder if the swelling didn't subside by the next morning. I was in intensive care for eleven days on the cancer ward. I guess they didn't have a snake bite floor! The good thing was that I had the complete attention of all the nurses, since I was the youngest person on the floor. Everybody else was much older than me…70s through 90s, so the nurses paid more attention to me, which was nice. I don't remember much, since they had me addicted to morphine to help alleviate the pain. I had a very good plastic surgeon. He told me he had to operate and remove part of my finger because it was pretty much useless at this point. Hemotoxins cause necrosis, which causes deterioration of the skin; it just eats it away. They had to pretty much cut away the majority of my middle finger and replace it with a piece of skin that they removed from my right wrist. The skin on my right middle finger actually belonged on my right wrist. I was released from the hospital two weeks later. I know that I died on January 27, 1987 and that

I’m one of the few people you will ever meet who has actually died twice!

Chapter Four

You Stole My Heart

To make matters worse and to show how bad my luck was back then, something else happened during my stay at the hospital while recovering from my rattlesnake bite. My parents drove hours to visit me almost daily. On one of my last days in intensive care, they were there, along with my roommate. She went in my mom's purse and stole one of her credit cards. My wallet had been stolen months earlier. I thought I was just out somewhere and someone had stolen it from my car, or it had fallen out of my pocket.

Well, my mom reported the credit card stolen and the Lansing police called them. My roommate had stolen the card and was trying to use it at a local K-Mart. It was my first day back home. I remember my mom calling me, crying, to let me know that Shay had just been arrested for theft. About 30 minutes later my door opened and the police entered with Shay in handcuffs. They were escorting her back to get some clothes and personal belongings. I was floored.

I had just been released from the hospital and had no use of my right hand. Now, my roommate, who was responsible for half of the bills, was being hauled away to jail for stealing my mom's credit card. I went through her things in her bedroom after she had been taken away and found my stolen wallet in her bottom drawer. She had been stealing from me the whole time she was there; I was too blind to see it. I couldn't work with just one hand and I now had to somehow cover all the bills by myself. The hospital bill alone was over $20,000. As always, my parents were there to help me out. I hope I'm half as good a parent to my kids as my parents have been to me!

Chapter Five

The Lion Sleeps Tonight

Back in April of 1993, I obtained my first African Black-Maned lion cub. I named him "Samson," because he was a male. I figured he was going to be pretty big and would warrant an impressive name. I had a one month old daughter to take care of and a 10-day-old lion. This was not easy to do. Samson had to be bottle fed every couple of hours around the clock with a special formula that I had to make up fresh for each feeding.

Three stories really stick out in my mind regarding Samson…one had to do with my dad and the other two had to do with Samson almost killing me. Samson weighed almost 650 pounds when he was fully grown and was one of the largest lions in the United States. He has since fathered 42 cubs that we know of at his home in a Wisconsin Zoo.

Let's go back to 1995 for the first story. Samson was housed in a giant enclosure inside our 20,000 square foot building where I ran my business…pretty close to the Detroit Metropolitan Airport. I was out of town, so my employees were taking care of my animals until I returned. I had an alarm system in place, which not only had verbal sirens on all the doors and windows, but also had motion detectors. My girlfriend got a phone call in the middle of the night from the alarm company saying that one of the motion detectors had been tripped inside near the back bay door. Since none of the door or window sensors went off, the alarm company assumed that something inside had escaped. What's large enough to set off a motion detector? A fully grown lion! Who does my girlfriend call since I am out of town? The police? Nope…she called my 60-year-old father.

My dad, who has always been there whenever I've needed him, got dressed, put on his boots and loaded his gun. He had a concealed weapons permit and he carried a .38 Special, not the most powerful of guns. He placed it in his holster and drove over to pick up my girlfriend. They drove all the way out to my warehouse. I can only guess what their 45-minute conversation entailed.

Once there, they had to pass through two glass doors and then two wooden doors to enter the hallway that led to the back of the building. There was a steel door that separated the back from the front and that is where Samson was housed. I have no idea what my dad was thinking or what he was planning to do with his little "pea shooter" had he encountered a 600 plus pound lion. Had he shot Samson, it just would have made the lion angry and one wouldn't like Samson when he was angry.

My dad entered first, of course, and opened up the steel door and turned on the lights. He heard Samson growling…not really growling, but wailing, just like we have probably heard lions do. My dad started walking back, waiting to be pounced upon. Luckily, to his surprise, he saw Samson still locked inside of his cage. My dad and my girlfriend searched the whole building and couldn't find anything loose and no cages were opened. The only thing that we can figure that set off the motion detector was probably a mouse or rat that might have escaped. I just thought that was a pretty funny story that my dad went there to protect everything from a fully grown African lion…with a .38 Special, in the middle of the night. I love you dad!

Chapter Six

I'm Tired

The second story that involved Samson pertained to me. Had I not had one of my employees with me that day, then I firmly believe that I would not be here right now telling this story. I don't remember what day it was, but I do remember that it was summer of 1995. Samson liked to destroy things; that's what lions do. Picture a cat scratching the furniture. Now picture a huge cat scratching the furniture. We used to get Samson old couches to play with. We would obtain them from people who were throwing them out and then put them in his cage to rip apart. He could shred a couch in about five minutes.

Other toys were truck tires from big rigs…you know, the giant tires that take three people to lift. We would roll one of them in his cage and he would swipe at it and knock it over. He would then pick it up in his mouth and shake it like a puppy would shake a stuffed animal! His favorite toys were old bowling balls. We had a local bowling alley that would donate their chipped 16 pound bowling balls they no longer used. I would insert my fingers into the bowling balls and actually bowl them into Samson's cage. He would stop the ball with his massive paws and then sink his teeth into them. I don't mean put his teeth into the existing three holes…I mean he would make additional holes by biting right into the polyurethane balls! He had so much power in his jaws that he would eventually just break the bowling balls into little pieces.

The thing about lions that most people don't know is that we don't mess with them when they have a new toy. We can't go near them because they are extremely possessive. Samson would pounce on these balls and couches, growl and show his teeth. I went in with him every day as I was the only one with a key to his cage. I wouldn't allow anyone else to ever go into his cage…even I knew enough not to try and enter when he had a new toy. I didn't trust him and I never turned my back on him (except for one time about which I will tell in the next chapter), even though I was his "dad" and I raised him since he was 10-days old. When he had a new toy, I didn't mess with him. I can't stress that enough!

Well, one day I took a semitruck tire and rolled it into his cage. When I thought he was done playing with it, I went into his cage to clean his litter box. He had a 500-pound litter box; he was a cat, right? I put 10 fifty-pound bags of kitty litter in once a week. As soon as I passed by him on my way to the trough, he did something that he had never done before. I have no doubt in my mind that he was going to kill me. He was protecting his new toy and I knew that I was trapped between him and the door. Luckily, one of my employees was working nearby and she came over when she saw what was going on. Had it not been for her, I truly believe that I wouldn't be here now. That was the only time in my entire life that I was ever afraid of an animal! Kim saw what was going on and she started running back and forth across the front of his cage to distract him. A cat's instinct is to chase. Kim ran and Samson chased her along the fence while I made my run to the door and got out before he realized what I was doing. It was extremely close and I learned a valuable lesson about big cats and their toys.

Chapter Seven

Litter Mates

The only time that Samson actually hurt me was when I was cleaning his litter box. He could have killed me but chose not to. This is where I learned to never turn my back on any animal, no matter how tame or trained I thought it was.

First, I need to describe his cage. It was fenced on all four sides with the backside being up against a concrete wall. The horse trough (litter box) was against the back wall. I had bent over to clean his litter box with a shovel when he came up behind me to play. I didn't see him sneaking up on me. I had no reason to look back since I trusted him. I bent over and he took his right paw and slapped me on my behind. He hit me with such force that it put my head into the cement wall, knocking me unconscious. Samson could have done anything he wanted to me since I was passed out on his floor.

I remember waking up to this really hard, sandpaper thing licking my face. Samson knew that something was wrong and he kept licking me to try and wake me up. I had a pretty bad bump on my head. I will never forget how close I came to dying once again. Since that day, I have never turned my back on him or any animal. I learned to respect animals and to know the damage they can do

Chapter Eight

Dog Day Afternoon

Who says dogs aren't dangerous? I had a major animal accident in September of 2001. At the time we had two adult Great Danes, a female (Xena) that was 165 pounds and a male (Merlin) who was 238 pounds. He was one of the largest Danes in the country and Xena was exceptionally large for a female.

I was outside around dusk and it was pretty hard to see. Xena was outside running and I was outside talking to my girlfriend. She called Xena because we couldn't see her and had no idea where she was in the darkness. Keep in mind that this dog weighed as much as an adult person. Xena came running at full speed toward my girlfriend's voice since. After all, Xena was her baby. Xena didn't see me standing about 10 feet in front of my girlfriend. I was wearing blue jeans and a black shirt, which made me pretty hard to see at night. Xena barreled into my left leg at full speed. She hit me with such force that she caused both of my legs to go over my head, sort of like me doing a somersault in mid air. One can imagine how much force that would take to flip a 200 pound adult man completely upside down in the air. I landed on the ground. Xena must have sustained a concussion from the force of the blow because she was in shock. She didn't know what she had hit, so she started jumping on me and attacking me while I lay on the ground. I don't remember much, nor do I remember the pain, because I went into shock.

I found out later, in the hospital, that my tibia (shinbone) was shattered. They said it wasn't just fractured, but that it was shattered like an egg shell. The ER doctor said it looked like a semitruck had plowed into my leg. My girlfriend got Xena off of me and I remember trying to stand up twice, but I just couldn't do it. My leg wouldn't work. I somehow crawled over to the cement steps leading up to our porch and asked my girlfriend to call 911.

I had never been in an ambulance in my life, but I had no choice since I couldn't stand. The ambulance arrived and the medics put me on a stretcher and took me to the hospital where my leg was x-rayed. I remember them telling me that I would need emergency surgery. I called up a very well-known surgeon who had worked on my arm before (alligator attack....will talk about it in a later chapter). Her name is Dr. Germaine Fritz and she is one of the best! She worked me in for emergency surgery the following day at Botsford Hospital. She said that my leg was so badly damaged that she had to remove part of my tibia and replace it with a cadaver bone. I remember signing the paperwork okaying a deceased person's bone be placed in my leg. They were hoping that my tibia would grow and attach to this cadaver bone. They also had to insert two steel plates and some screws in my leg to hold the bones in place. I was told that there was a good chance that I would never walk again. I got out of the hospital the following day and was in extreme pain. I had to use a wheelchair for over six months.

But wait…there's more! I realized that something was wrong with my leg about one week after I came home from the hospital. The pain was so intense that I had to call an ambulance again. They rushed me back to the hospital and it turned out that I had a blood clot in my foot, which they told me could be life threatening. I didn't need surgery, but they placed me on dangerous blood thinners and told me that if I cut myself that I could bleed to death. Oh, how the good news piles up!

But wait…there's even more! A couple weeks later I awoke to incredible pain…the most intense pain you could ever feel. My leg was burning up. It hurt so much that I couldn't even have a sheet over it. My leg had turned black…I'm talking from my knee to the tip of my toes was jet black. I went to a specialist! When the nurse came into the exam room, she said my leg was "too gross to look at" and that she had to leave the room. Boy, did that make me feel good. The doctor came in and didn't know what was wrong with my leg, so he sent me to another specialist…and another specialist…and another. I don't remember how many I ended up going to see until I was finally diagnosed with RSD. RSD stands for Reflex Sympathetic Dystrophy, which is the most painful disease known to man. Many people have been known to commit suicide because of the incredible pain. There are also documented cases of people amputating their own limbs because of the pain and then suffering from phantom pain in their non-existent limbs…extremely painful!

I was put on two different narcotics and ended up having to get three nerve blocks in my back. RSD is rarely curable. It might go into remission in a few cases but it usually comes back. Trauma is what sets it off. All said and done, I finally overcame the RSD but ended up getting RLS, which stands for Restless Leg Syndrome. Many people have this. Your leg(s) involuntarily moves, usually while sleeping. It looks like you are riding an imaginary bicycle in your sleep. I still have RLS, but the RSD hasn't resurfaced in about six years.

The doctors don't know what causes RLS, but I'm pretty sure it had nothing to do with the dog running into my leg. I was in rehab for over six months; I can now use my leg and do almost anything. I can't kneel on my left knee and it hurts in extreme temperatures. I'm guessing it's from the steel in there. OK, that's my dog story. Of all the exotic and dangerous animals that I have dealt with, look at what happened from a dog!

Chapter Nine

Snake in The Grass

My job enables me to work with many police agencies. They call me when they encounter someone who has an illegal or dangerous animal since I'm trained to capture and restrain almost any type. I also have the means to house pretty much anything until we can find it an appropriate home at a zoo or another sanctuary.

Well, three years ago, I received a call for help from a police department in Oregon. They had busted a drug house and confiscated an adult Rhinoceros viper and an eight-foot long Forest cobra. I have never had a Forest cobra, so I did some research on them and found out that they are the second largest venomous snake, second only to the King cobra and that their bite is usually fatal. They are responsible for more deaths in Africa than all other venomous snakes. The police asked if I would take these snakes, or they would have to euthanize them. They couldn't find any suitable facility closer to them and I was their last resort. I said sure, since we are a non-profit exotic animal rescue and we don't turn away any animal, no matter how dangerous. It's not the animal's fault that it ended up as a pet in someone's house.

The authorities flew these two snakes into Detroit Metropolitan Airport where I picked them up. I found a home for the Rhino viper at a licensed educational facility in Washington. I decided to keep the Forest cobra for use in our shows when I perform on stage for large crowds. I would never bring him out in a small venue…only when I'm on a large stage where there is no danger of anyone else getting injured. He is great for educating people about what kind of animal NOT to get!

I was headlining the Columbus Pet Expo in 2008 and I brought him along. I travel with him in a sealed Rubbermaid tub that is escape proof. I arrived at our hotel in Columbus as I always arrive a day early to get situated and set-up. I carted all the animals into our room. One can only imagine the stares we get when walking through the lobby with all these unusual animals. I always keep them with me so I can make sure they are properly taken care of. Also, most of them are nocturnal and need to be fed at night, so I would never leave them at an Expo Center. They always travel with me, wherever I go. It's a lot of fun to stay in a hotel room with me…one never knows what could happen!

I cracked open the cobra's container, once we were situated in our room, and saw that he had decided to go to the bathroom sometime during our four-hour drive. I don't know how many of you have ever smelled an 8 foot cobra's poop, but I can pretty much guarantee that if you ever do, you will never forget it…it reeks! He was covered in poop, the container was covered in poop and now I was covered in poop! I had no choice other than to give him a bath and scrub out his container in the hotel bathroom.

I brought five employees with me and one of them was my 21-year-old nephew, Russ. Everyone had their own hotel room except for me. I shared my room with my wife, our four-month old son and all of our animals that had accompanied us to the Expo. I went to all my employees' rooms and told them not to come into our room until I gave the OK, because the cobra would be loose while I cleaned out his cage and gave him a bath. Picture this…my wife was lying on the bed with our son while I carried the cobra's container into the bathroom.

I filled the bathtub with luke warm water so the cobra could soak while I cleaned his crate. I used a large snake hook to remove him from his container and placed him into the bathtub. I had to watch him closely to make sure he didn't slither back out and try to bite me. I had the bathroom door shut so he couldn't escape but it wasn't locked in case he bit me and I needed assistance. While he was soaking in the bathtub, I had to turn around to use the sink to clean out his crate.

I was in the middle of cleaning it when someone knocked on the bathroom door. It was Russ. He knew what I was doing and he wanted to see how it was going. He cracked the door open before I could tell him not to enter because the cobra was in the bathtub.

Before Russ could enter, I heard the bathtub water start to run. I looked over to my right as Russ opened the door. The cobra had slithered up the wall and had his neck wrapped around the shower head, while his tail had wrapped around the hot water faucet turning it on.

Now one must realize what I was dealing with: I didn't want the bathtub overflowing, I didn't want the scalding hot water burning the cobra; I couldn't just turn off the handle because his head would be right above me; I now had Russ halfway in the bathroom, because he had no idea of what was happening. Russ got to see the cobra completely stretched out between the shower head and the faucet. I managed to turn the hot water off, while keeping a close eye on his head. I then proceeded to unwrap his tail from the faucet while trying to avoid getting bitten. I turned on the cold water to neutralize the hot water that had gone into the tub and I used the snake hook to place the cobra back in the water and get him all cleaned up.

I made sure to run and grab my camera to get photos of this fiasco that can be seen elsewhere in this book. This is one of my nephew's favorite stories to tell people…him opening the bathroom door and seeing this gigantic cobra stretched out while turning on the water in the bathtub.

Chapter Ten

See Ya Later, Alligator

I met a gentleman in August, 2007 while performing at a baseball game for the Lansing Lugnuts. He asked for one of my cards and he told me that he was a police officer for Northville Township, Michigan and that he would keep my card, in case they ever needed my help. He didn't think he would ever need my assistance since nothing exciting ever happens in Northville Township.

I received a phone call from him less than two weeks later while I was cleaning cages in our sanctuary. He said that they needed my assistance. I asked him why and he stated that they had a nine-foot alligator loose in a local parking lot. I asked him if he personally saw it and he said that he was on his way to the scene. I asked him to call me when he got there, because many people exaggerate. It was an hour drive each way for me. I had to know what to bring to capture this beast and it all depended on its size.

My phone rang about 20 minutes later and he said, "Mark, we need you to come out here." I asked him how large and he said it was the biggest alligator he had ever seen! He gave me directions to the police department and Channel 2 was waiting there when I arrived. Obviously, someone had tipped them off. I went inside and was told that two guys from Detroit, who both had bench warrants out for their arrests, thought they were invincible and decided to take their "little" pet for a stroll. This was a six-seven foot alligator with a spiked pit bull dog collar around his neck that they had affectionately named "Beefy-T Bad Boy."

They had just arrived at a local pet store and were walking in from the parking lot when a few employees spotted them. One of the men had Beefy-T slung over his shoulder, sort of like you would carry a baseball bat or a sack of potatoes and the alligator's mouth was not taped shut. I was told that they transported him there in the trunk of their car. The people in the pet store became scared, locked the doors and called the police, who then called me.

When the police arrived, they surrounded these guys but didn't know what to do. It was a one-hour drive for me to get there, so they decided to take the 'gator back to the police precinct. They weren't going to go near this monster, so they had the owners place it in the back seat of one of their squad cars. The police were going to arrest both of these men for having an illegal animal, since owning an alligator is against the law. Alligators are not pets, and no one in the history of the world, has ever raised an alligator to an adult and kept it friendly. It can't be done! The alligator's only predators are humans…they are that high up on the food chain! We've probably receive more calls to rescue alligators than all other animals combined!

There was footage on numerous television stations of these two guys trying to put this 'gator in the back seat of the police car. They wanted him in, and he didn't want to go. Guess who won? Beefy-T, of course! You can see the one man wrestling with him and losing, eventually backing out of the police car. The officers had him put Beefy-T back in their trunk, so they could escort them all to the police station until I arrived.

I showed up not knowing what to expect. Beefy-T was loose in a holding cell for me to handle. Both men were arrested and placed in a jail cell, and the police led me to the other cell where the 'gator was being held. I asked them to unlock the door so I could get in, and not to open it again until I told them that I had the 'gator secured. I entered and then realized that Beefy-T was not too happy. Now, one must picture this: These are big, well-trained police officers who all had weapons on them…clubs, guns and tasers. They led me to the jail cell and I noticed that there was only one door and no windows. There was no furniture, just a cement slab that could be used as a bed. That's it!

This large alligator was extremely stressed out… unfamiliar environment, unfamiliar people and no owners. Alligators have no fear and no predators in the wild, except for man. So, it's me and this large alligator in a jail cell. The officers were in the hallway, but they couldn't see what was going on. I went to grab him; he turned and tried to bite me. I jumped up on the concrete slab and one of the officers mistakenly thought that I had the 'gator secured. He opened the door right as I yelled that I didn't have him yet. I told him to shut the door until I gave the OK.

I grabbed Beefy-T with both hands, jumped on his back to restrain him and that's when I realized that I had left my transport container back in the lobby. I picked up Beefy-T with both arms and tried to secure him as best I could. I didn't have any help, because none of the officers were going anywhere near me. Again, one must picture these guys…seven trained officers who are fearless. They weren't afraid of dangerous thugs with weapons or people who were high on drugs. These guys were fearless! Well, they saw me coming out of the cell with this alligator and every single one of them, except for the one who had the door, took off running down the hall! The officer who opened the door for me stayed there because he was hiding behind it.

I walked down the hall and went into the lobby where the T.V. cameras were waiting. The police wouldn't allow them in the back where the cells were, but they had every right to be in the lobby. They taped me putting the 'gator in the travel container, and I later found out that it made national news. A friend of mine is a sheriff in Minnesota; he called me when he saw it on his local news, as did one of my old employees, who now resides in California. Ron Savage was the Detroit journalist who covered the story and he did a really good job. His closing line of the story was perfect. As I successfully placed Beefy-T in the carrier and was closing the lid, he laughed and said, "See ya later, alligator.

Chapter Eleven

I Have To Go Potty

Another Beefy-T Bad Boy story occurred in March of 2009 when I was headlining the Columbus Pet Expo. My wife, son and I headed back to our hotel room after my performances on Friday. I had three hotel rooms for our employees and us, but no extra room for the animals. They had to stay in our room. Since Beefy-T Bad Boy is a large, potentially deadly alligator, I didn't want to chance his escaping at night while we were sleeping. Remember, my wife and our one-year-old son were also in the room. I put Beefy-T's travel carrier (with him in it) in the bathroom and closed the door. I also had an eight foot cobra with me and decided to lock him in the bathroom also, just to be safe.

Well, my wife awoke in the middle of the night to use the bathroom. She opened the bathroom door, turned on the light, while still half asleep, only to see Beefy-T looking right up at her just inside the door. He escaped from his crate and was just waiting at the door. My wife was very calm…not happy, but calm. She turned the lights off, shut the door and went back to bed, not wanting to wake me. She ended up holding it in, just so I could get a good night's rest. How many of your spouses would do the same for you?

She told me what had happened when I awakened in the morning. I opened the door to check, and sure enough, there was a large alligator loose in our bathroom! Since I was running late, I just stepped over him, used the bathroom, took a shower and put him back in his crate. Then my wife used the bathroom.

Chapter Twelve

The Cowz Jumped Over the Moon

This is one of my favorite stories. I have changed the name of the man in this story since we don't turn in people. We care more about the animals' well-beings than getting someone in trouble. Everything else is completely true.

I received a phone call in August, 2007 from a lady that lived in a trailer park. She told me that she had seen my shows before, knew my reputation, and needed my help. I had no idea who she was, but I asked her what I could do to help. She said that Carl, a neighbor of hers, had a giant alligator living in his mobile home. She had seen it through his window. She was worried about the safety of all the kids and other people in her trailer park, since this alligator was just walking around loose in Carl's trailer. It seemed that Carl had raised it from a hatchling over 15 years ago.

She wanted me to come out and confiscate his alligator. I explained to her that I'm not a police officer and that I don't have the authority to take animals from people. I told her that if Carl wanted to call me himself and relinquish it, that I would come out and take his alligator to our sanctuary, where we would find it an appropriate home at a zoo. I would ask no questions since we don't turn in people.

Now, if the police were to find out about Carl, they would most likely arrest him and then call us. After much talking, she finally convinced him to call me. Carl asked if I would come out and rescue his alligator. He was only about a 45-minute drive. The alligator's name was "Cowz." Carl really didn't want to give him up, since he lived alone. Cowz was his baby. He had recently lost his job, had no money coming in, and couldn't really afford to take care of Cowz anymore. He made me promise to find Cowz a good home at a zoo, because I told him that I wasn't going to keep an alligator that large. It just wasn't safe, as they always turn on you.

He gave me directions to his trailer park. I took an eight-foot horse trough with me to transport his alligator. I had no idea how large it was! Carl said it was pretty big, but the majority of people I have dealt with tend to exaggerate. I knocked on his screen door and he called out for me to come in. I have never seen anything like what I am about to describe. Had I not witnessed this with my own eyes, then I wouldn't have believed it. I will swear on a stack of Bibles that everything you are about to read is true.

I opened the door and walked in. The only thing separating me from the largest alligator I have ever dealt with in my life was a couch. Cowz was loose and just resting on the floor. He had to have been 10-12 feet long and well over 200 pounds! Carl had no money for air conditioning, so all of his windows were wide open. Remember, this was August and extremely hot outside…close to 100 degrees on this particular day. The only thing stopping this monstrous alligator from getting outside and eating any of the children who were playing, were the window screens!

Now, Carl told me that he hadn't fed Cowz yet and he wanted to know if he should feed him before I took him. I wanted to see what he was going to do so, I told him to go ahead and feed him. Carl then told me that Cowz had only eaten canned cat food his entire life. He ate two large cans of food per day. I muttered, "Ok, cool." I was thinking this guy was completely insane. He opened up one can of cat food, and while I was still standing between the couch and the 'gator, he knelt right in front of Cows (about two inches from his mouth) and asked, "Cowz, want some num-nums?" Again, I witnessed this with my own eyes. Cowz slowly opened his mouth really wide and Carl used his hand to scoop out a chunk of canned cat food and proceeded to toss it into the 'gator's mouth. Cowz snapped his mouth shut and Carl scooped out another chunk. Keep in mind that he was kneeling directly in front of Cowz. Carl wasn't quick enough getting the food out this time, and Cowz took a snap and almost got his knee. Carl took a step back and slapped Cowz on the nose and scolded, "Bad Cowz, Bad Cowz. That's not your num-nums. Now, do you want your num-nums?" Again, I kid you not, Cowz reopened his mouth and Carl threw the rest of the can of cat food into his mouth.

It was right at this point that I started thinking to myself that I was going to become famous. I would be on every TV show with this giant alligator eating right out of my hands. Remember, this guy just hit him on his snout and Cowz did nothing except wait patiently for his food. Carl told me that Cowz didn't have a cage and that he slept under his bed at night. Carl also said that he was awakened many mornings to find Cowz lying on the bed next to him. Carl mentioned that he had a shower with curtains, not glass doors, and that Cowz got into the tub with him while he was taking a shower. Again, I was thinking how lucky I was and that this was going to be an incredible story.

Have you figured out where this story is going yet? OK, I'll tell you. I still hadn't gone near Cowz, but I asked Carl if he knew how we were going to get Cowz outside, since he weighed hundreds of pounds. I told him I had a horse trough with me and he suggested that I bring it in, because he didn't want any of his neighbors to see Cowz. I still couldn't believe that he had been living here with an alligator for 15 years with no one finding out until now. I went out to my van and brought the horse trough back in, only to see that Cowz was now gone. Carl said that Cowz became scared and ran back into the bedroom. So, now I'm thinking, "Great, now I have to go get him." I asked Carl what he wanted me to do and he said that he would go get him. I wasn't about to argue!

Carl disappeared down the hall and came back out of the bedroom struggling with his giant alligator because of the weight. Carl put him in the horse trough and Cowz had to curl his tail around because he was much longer than the eight-foot trough. I grabbed the tail end of the trough (I'm no dummy!) and Carl got the head end. We lifted the horse trough and proceeded to carry it to my van.

Now, I don't know how much you know about reptiles, so I'll explain something to you. The majority of them need the ultraviolet rays found in natural sunlight to thrive. Usually, when a reptile is not exposed to sunlight at all and then gets to bask in the sun, they change and do a Linda Blair (kids, ask your parents). Well, we got Cowz outside and he started carrying on a little bit when the sun hit him. I lifted the horse trough into the back of my van and threw a piece of screen that I had over it…like that's going to do any good if he decided he wanted out! I wasn't worried because I now had the calmest alligator in the world!

I drove out of the trailer park and called my wife, because I was so excited. I said, "Honey, you're not going to believe me, but this the largest alligator I have ever dealt with." Of course she thought I was joking, since I'm always messing around. I said, "He's incredible!" I proceeded to tell her about Carl hand feeding him and slapping him, when he almost lost his knee to Cowz' massive jaws. I looked in my rear-view mirror, while I was telling her this, and observed that Cowz no longer wanted to be in the metal trough. He pushed up the screen and his head was now touching the ceiling of my high-top conversion van. For those of you who don't know how tall that is, I can stand back there and not hit my head on the roof! I yelled, "I gotta go…he's out!" I hung up the phone trying to figure out what I was going to do, when he came up near me while I was driving. I pulled over and went to the back. Cowz had fallen back into the horse trough. Now he was trying to kill me! I guess the sun's rays had taken effect and he was freaking out. I put random items that I had in the back of my van on top of the screen to try and hold it down while I drove home.

I arrived back at our sanctuary and drove to a large outdoor pen with a pond. I was going to put Cowz in it to temporarily hold him until I could find a zoo that would take him. I walked up to the house to get my wife and daughter. I told them that they had to come out and see this monster. It's the largest alligator I have ever seen in person and my wife, knowing my sense of humor, thought that I had just come home with a little two-foot alligator, since most of the calls we received were gross exaggerations. She thought I was just messing around, because most of the calls we got for giant snakes turned out to be pretty small. She brought the video camera expecting to see a tiny alligator. She looked in the rear window of the van and freaked out. Cowz was not in a good mood and my wife said that I was crazy if I thought she was going to help me get him out. My wife is an awesome woman, and she pretty much lets me do what I want, but the only animals she hugely fears are alligators and crocodiles.

My 15- year-old daughter came with us to help me get Cowz out of the van. Jessica is like me and will pretty much do anything. I got the head end while she got the tail end. Now remember, he was extremely heavy. We pulled the trough out of the van while Cowz was trying to bite us the entire time. My wife captured all of this with the video camera, while keeping a safe distance. We got it near the pen where it was to be temporarily housed, and I told my daughter to put the tail end down. I didn't want her anywhere near it when I took the screen off. I put my end down at the door to the pen and I went around to the far end (the one my daughter had) to lift it and try to get Cowz to come out and walk right into the pen. He turned as he came out and snapped at my right arm. My wife captured all of this on film and it was at this point that she said she realized that I was completely nuts. I don't know why it took her so long to come to that conclusion!

I found him a home at an alligator sanctuary in Missouri where he would spend the rest of his life with 62 other alligators. I gave Cowz to them with the understanding that he would live out the rest of his life there. I had to drive him all the way down there, 604 miles each way, and I needed to make sure he couldn't escape or move around much during the ride so as to accidently injure himself. I ended up having to build a wooden crate to transport him.

The crate that I built had to be custom made specifically for Cowz. It couldn't be wide enough for him to turn around or he could get injured. I had to measure Cowz at his widest part and measure his length and then build a crate this was almost exactly that size. I needed to get him to enter head first and make him crawl forward until he was completely in. That way he couldn't injure himself nor could he turn around to injure me. The trick was getting his head into the opening and then getting him to walk forward instead of backward. I built the crate and put it inside the pen where Cowz was. There were four doors that went into this pen and I entered the door furthest from him. I put the crate down and faced the opening nearest him. I then figured that I had to get near him and guide him into the crate, while at the same time avoiding his tail and jaws. Oh yeah, I forgot to mention that there were 7 other alligators in this pen with him! He was the largest by far, but the others ranged from three to about seven feet…all large enough to do quite a bit of damage. I jumped on his back and pinned his head down so he couldn't open his mouth. I then had to literally ride him toward the crate, all the time making sure he didn't throw me off or get his jaws open. I also had to make sure that the other 'gators didn't get me. Cowz definitely didn't want to go in the crate. It took me about 30-45 minutes of wrestling with him to finally get his head into the open end. Once his head was in he could no longer open his mouth or turn around to bite me. All I had to do was keep him going straight instead of backing up and it worked perfectly.

Not only did it cost us money to feed and house him, as we had him for about three months, but I ended up spending our own money for gas to drive to Missouri and back, as well as on the materials to build the crate to transport him. However, the story has a happy ending. My daughter and I drove him down to the zoo in Missouri where he still lives contently with 62 other alligators!

Chapter Thirteen

The Bear Necessities

I remember when I got my first bear, back in 1991, a baby black bear we named Boo Boo. I bottle raised him and he thanked me by putting me in the hospital to get stitched up after he ripped open my right arm with his massive claws. You're probably picturing a full grown bear attacking me, right? He did all this damage while he was still a cub! He wanted his bottle and I guess I didn't get it to him fast enough. He saw it coming and he started growling and scratching me to get to it. I still have the scars on my right arm as proof.

I received a phone call a few months later to do a television commercial. It was for Dodge Caravan and they wanted me to bring an adult black bear to the shoot. I had a three-year-old female bear named Cindy, but I thought it would be easier to work with my cub. They agreed and I brought Boo Boo to the set. I figured this would be a piece of cake and that we would be out of there in about an hour or so. However, once they saw him they had to re write the script. They originally wanted a ferocious adult bear so they had to re write the script to show a really cute baby bear. They wanted me to make him beg and look extremely cute. I tried, but no matter what I did, he wouldn't cooperate. All he wanted to do was explore the set and play.

I then got the brilliant idea to get him some marshmallows. Boo Boo was about 100-125 pounds at the time and my idea was to climb on top of a ladder and dangle a marshmallow, so he would get on his hind legs and beg for it. The camera was on a rig above me, so it was aimed down at Boo Boo. Well, we did so many takes that he went through the whole bag of marshmallows. We're not talking a little baggie of mini-marshmallows; we're talking a full size bag of large marshmallows!

I wasn't thinking about the consequences of a bear on a sugar rush. It was the last thing in the world that anybody should have to endure. Well, the sugar started to affect Boo Boo and, he became extremely hyper and uncooperative. The director told me to take him in a back room and calm him down. We went into a dressing room and we sat there for about two hours. Boo Boo was literally running back and forth bashing his head into the walls and into me. He wasn't hurting himself; he was just playing. Finally, he calmed down enough for us to do a couple more takes. We eventually got their ideal footage!.

Chapter Fourteen

Up Your Nose with a Rubber Hose

I obtained another bear, Cindy, from a friend in Chicago who used her for some television commercials. He said that they weren't really using her anymore, so I agreed to take her. My buddy drove Cindy down to me. I was pretty impressed with her size; ok….scared is a much more appropriate adjective to use! Cindy weighed about 300 pounds and was taller than me. She was as friendly as a bear could possibly be. She loved walking around on her hind legs and made sure to always give me a bear hug first thing in the morning.

I constructed a giant pen for Cindy and Boo Boo; they became the best of friends. Steve, who was one of my employees, came in one day soon after I acquired Cindy. He had no idea that she was loose in the back of our sanctuary. He disliked bears because Boo Boo would chase him around the warehouse when I let him out…Boo Boo, not Steve! Boo Boo loved to torment Steve. Cindy, on the other hand, liked Steve; in fact, she liked everybody.

One particular day, Steve walked to the back of our sanctuary and Cindy was loose. He had no idea that there was a full-grown bear back there, let alone a loose one. Cindy ran up to him, and Steve, not being the biggest guy, had no idea what to do. He froze in terror!

Cindy rose up on her hind legs and put her paws around the back of his neck. She towered over him and opened her mouth. Steve was sure that he was about to be a bear snack. There was absolutely nothing he could do. He was too scared to yell or move, so he just stood there and closed his eyes waiting for the inevitable. It happened all right. Cindy leaned into Steve and stuck her tongue up his nose and started licking his face. That was Steve's first experience with an adult black bear and I believe it was his last.

I donated Boo Boo and Cindy to a bear sanctuary in Pennsylvania once I determined that they needed a larger place. I drove to visit them two years later and asked the curator if I could get into their cage. He said that no one had gone into their cage since the day he brought them to Pennsylvania from my place. He told me that if I was crazy enough to go in a cage with two adult black bears that probably didn't even remember me, then to go ahead.

I walked in and Cindy immediately ran over to me and gave me a huge bear hug. Boo Boo, who was now a full-grown monster, came over as Cindy was licking me. He wasn't as nice. He chased me around a few hay bales and I barely (get it?) made it out of their cage alive. I decided it was just as well to pet him through the bars.

Chapter Fifteen

The Scum of the Earth

Something awful occurred during the night of February 9, 2007 that changed my life and my family's life forever! I awoke the morning of February 10, 2007 and walked to my sanctuary at 8 a.m. We have a 10-acre sanctuary, and our house is located at the front. We had been living there since 1995 and I have never locked the doors. We had three huge Great Danes at the time and no one had ever come onto our property unannounced before. I had always been a trusting person and never had a reason to lock the doors.

I went to open the door and couldn't turn the handle…it was locked. I knew I hadn't locked it, and I had to walk back up to the house to get the key. I unlocked the door and entered the building. Everything seemed normal, at first, until I realized that our sloth's cage was empty. Again, I didn't really comprehend what had happened, until I noticed that her travel crate, the one I always kept on top of her cage, was also missing. It was at that very moment that my heart sank and my life was turned upside down!

Seven, our sloth, was gone! Someone had broken in and taken her. I continued to look around in disbelief, and saw that Peek-a-boo, our joey, was also gone, and that her cage door was shut. Her cage was directly across from Seven's. She slept inside of a custom made pouch, sort of like a purse, that hung in one corner of her cage. The pouch, with her inside it, was gone.

I was in shock and didn't know what to do. I walked back up to our house to tell my wife what had happened and called the Sumpter Township Police on the way. Diane and I went back to the sanctuary to see if anything else was missing, and we found numerous animals were stolen…our giant African Pixie frog, an adult Pink-Toe tarantula, and our whole colony of rare walking sticks, over 100 of them. They were the largest species in the world, and some of them were almost two-feet long!

The police arrived and took our statements. I had them call the Detroit Metropolitan Airport and alert the cargo departments, just in case someone tried to ship out any exotic animals. We told the police everything, and I remember saying to one of the detectives, "Whoever did this will probably return them when they find out they don't have the means to care for them." He told me he had never heard of any criminal returning what they had stolen…never! Keep reading and you will see how that statement came back to haunt me!

I then told the police that something wasn't right about this. Why would someone come in, steal the animals, and then lock the door on the way out? Why would they close the cage doors after removing the animals? It didn't make sense, unless they were used to doing that. The policemen thought someone with knowledge of our sanctuary might be responsible, so they immediately called the Romulus Police Department and had them issue a search warrant for one of our helpers.

They had me accompany them to her house, where five Romulus Police cars were waiting. They had each end of the street blocked off, and her house was surrounded. The police and I knocked on her door, and she let us in. She said she had nothing to hide, and we could search wherever we wanted. The police checked everywhere, including her attic and barn, and turned up nothing.

I went home and became extremely depressed…I couldn't even sleep anymore. I had awful nightmares and awoke, almost nightly, in a cold sweat. You could see our sanctuary from our bedroom window, and I would continuously sit up in bed and stare out our window, thinking someone was out there.

I contacted the media, and several television and newspaper reporters arrived to cover the story. They showed photos of our stolen animals, and we put up a reward for any information leading to their whereabouts. A few of the stations ran the story over and over, to no avail. I became more worried and stressed as each day went by, because these animals required special diets. Wallabies can eat sweet potatoes, but can't eat white potatoes. They can eat wheat bread, but not white enriched bread. Most sloths love bananas, but Seven wouldn't touch any food in her bowl, if there was even one slice of banana in it.

I couldn't continue performing as usual, because Seven was a huge part of my presentations. People really looked forward to her, and she was the only animal that accompanied me to every one of my shows. My Animal Magic shirts even featured her on the front!

I started locking all our doors since that fateful night. I didn't trust anyone anymore, except my family, of course. I started to lose hope as more and more days, and then weeks, went by. We received no tips, and had no clue where to look. I did everything I could think of. I posted ads all over town and on the internet. I called zoos throughout the country and alerted them. My heart raced every time the phone rang, and would sink even further, when I found out that the call didn't pertain to our animals.

My daughter and I walked to our sanctuary on the morning of April 1st and noticed a crate laying on the ground near the door…Seven's crate! My mind started racing…I didn't know what to think. Was Seven in the crate? If so, was she alive? Was it just her head in the box? I had no clue. There was a reason for me thinking her head was in the box. There was a story in the paper two days earlier regarding a missing German Shepherd. The little girl, who owned the dog, received a wrapped box on her porch the morning of her birthday. When she opened it, she discovered her missing dog's head!

I thought it was the same people who had taken our sloth. I had my daughter run up to the house to get my wife, who was eight months pregnant at the time. What was I thinking…I called a pregnant woman to open the box to see what was inside. All she needed was to see Seven's head in there and our son would have been born prematurely!

I regained my composure when Diane arrived and told her not to open the box. I nudged it with my foot to see if it was empty, and felt some weight in it. I now knew that something was inside. I carefully lifted one corner and peeked in, seeing brown fur. I closed the lid, not knowing what to do next. I saw Seven was in there, but I still didn't know if she was alive. I took the lid completely off and we realized it was a sloth…not our sloth, but a sloth. Seven was the largest sloth in the United States, weighing 43 pounds when she was stolen. This sloth wasn't even half of that!

After further inspection, I noticed that it was indeed Seven. Seven had a deformed claw on her rear right leg, as did this one. She was extremely malnourished and scared to death. On top of that, we had freezing rain the previous night and that morning. Sloths are native to the rain forest in Brazil and need to be kept above 85 degrees all the time. We found out later, from our veterinarian, that Seven had pneumonia.

I called the Sumpter Township Police Department again, and they arrived within a few minutes. They assumed the thieves came back to take more animals, and they brought Seven back because she was near death. They couldn't get in this time because we had locked all the doors. The police guessed something had scared them off before they could break in. It looked like they had just thrown her on the ground and took off.

I put Seven back in her cage and tried to feed her, but she wouldn't eat. Her favorite foods were corn-on-the-cob and peanuts, and she wouldn't even eat them. I weighed her. She weighed 21 pounds, less than half her normal weight! I tried for days to feed her, with no success, but I could tell she was improving. She would come to the door of her cage whenever I walked by, like she was happy to be back.

She eventually took a piece of sweet potato from my hand. I was ecstatic! I fed her a little more each time I walked by. I weighed her every day to make sure she wasn't still losing weight. The only way I could get her to eat was to hand feed her. She still wouldn't eat out of a bowl, but I was making progress. She started to put on weight and finally ate on her own, after over two months of hand-feeding by my wife and me.

Ok, flash back to a couple of days after Seven was returned. I got the shock of my life when the detective who investigated the first robbery showed up at our door. He brought me to his squad car and asked me a lot of questions. He wanted to know where I was the night of the break in and other questions that seemed weird for him to be asking me. He told me he was bringing in one of my helpers to take a lie-detector test, and said I would need to take one also. I asked him why, and he said he had never seen a thief come back to the scene of their crime to return anything. He then told me that I had predicted my animals would be returned! Remember earlier, when I told you one of my statements would come back to haunt me? It did!

He scheduled my lie detector test for the following Monday, and I passed it with flying colors, as I knew I would. Kim passed hers also, which put the police back at square one…no suspects and no leads.

I hadn't slept well since that fateful day back in April, and I still had no idea who was responsible for our stolen animals. I missed Peek-a-boo tremendously. She was the sweetest wallaby I had ever raised, and she would even follow me around like a puppy.

History repeated itself on August 24, 2007. I went to work that morning and unlocked the door. The first cage I saw every morning housed Ben, my fennec fox. I notice he was missing, and I started calling his name. I figured he had somehow jumped out and was running around somewhere. As I walked down the hall searching for him, my heart sank again. I saw Wookie's cage door wide open. Wookie was my kinkajou, who I had bottle raised since the day he was born, 11 years earlier.

I realized that I had been robbed again. Two of my favorite animals were gone! I looked to see how they had gained entry and found one of my windows open with the screen lying on the ground outside. I once again called the Sumpter Township Police Department, and they showed up within a few minutes.

They dusted the window and screen and took fingerprints from both. We contacted the media, and they put us on television again, with the hope that someone would come forward with any information. Whoever did this turned my life upside down again. My daughters were now afraid to go outside at night, as they should have been. You see, they were sleeping outside in a tent the night of August 23rd. They could have been injured, kidnapped, or worse. I could no longer sleep through the night. I was worried that whoever did this would return and break into our house. The slightest noise would startle me, and I would think someone was trying to enter our home. I can't count how many nights I would awaken and run outside, positive that someone was trying to break in.

I was obsessed with finding the culprit, or culprits. I spent countless hours on-line every day searching web sites for anything that might be a lead. I typed the words: animals, magic, exotics, pets, and many others into different search engines, hoping for a break with no luck. My wife had been doing some on line searching also, and found a similar crime had been committed at the Birch Run Zoo in Michigan. She called them and found out that someone used a bulldozer and broke through a fence during the night.

They stole three large African Spurred tortoises, two fennec foxes and a wallaby. The weird similarity was that the foxes' and the wallabies' cages were both closed after the animals were taken…same as ours!

Finally, at 7:38 a.m. on Halloween, something happened that I will never forget! I had performed another search, when a man popped up on my computer screen. I had no clue who he was, but I did recognize the animal on his shoulder…it was Wookie! I was positive, because Wookie looked unlike any other kinkajou I had ever seen. His nose was more pointed. I shouted for my wife, because I needed verification from someone else. I wanted it to be him so badly that maybe I was just imagining it.

My wife came running and looked at the computer screen. She started crying when she saw him and said that it was Wookie. That's all I needed to hear. I called the State Police and you'll never guess what they did. They hung up on me, after saying that I had no proof, other than a visual confirmation. The trooper asked me if Wookie had any tattoos and I told him no. He then asked me if Wookie was micro-chipped and I told him no. He then told me that he couldn't do anything on my assumption. I proceeded to talk to him and he hung up on me. Pretty nice, huh?

I did some more research on this guy I discovered on the internet and found his web site. He had copied and pasted some of my information on his web site and actually stole my identity. His name was Adam Locke and his partner was Joshua Roberts. They were calling themselves Those Animal Guys, and they were performing MY shows with MY animals!

Luckily, I work with many police departments, and I never ask for any compensation. When I get a call regarding an illegal, or dangerous animal, I usually drop whatever I'm doing and head out to their location. There is never any fee for the gas, time, wear and tear on my van, or anything else involved. I called in a favor to a Sumpter Township Policewoman, and she said she would see what she could do to help. She called me back and told me to call a Sergeant with the Livonia Police Department. She had already briefed him and checked out this web site I had given her. I called him and he said he would look into it. Finally, someone who could help us!

I received a call back from the sergeant on Sunday night, November 4th. He told me that they had surveillance on a house in Flint for the past three days, and there were animals in the house. They had no idea how many, or what type, but they wanted to know if I would accompany them with a search warrant, just in case they needed my help. I want to make it clear that I wasn't going with them because of my stolen animals. I was going to help them if they encountered dangerous or venomous animals.

The sergeant told me they were obtaining a search warrant, and that I should be prepared to go with when they called me. He also said not to tell anyone, so as not to tip off these people. I ended up telling my wife, who I knew I could trust, and waited patiently to hear from him. He called me the next day and said they had the warrant, and that I should meet them at the Livonia Police Department at 7 a.m. the following Tuesday morning.

I couldn't sleep Monday night, as usual, but for a different reason this time. There was a chance I could get Wookie, Peek-a-boo, Ben and my other animals back! I arrived at the Livonia Police Department at 6 a.m. and waited in my van. I had brought along pillow cases and snake hooks, in case there were reptiles, along with travel carriers and aquariums. I went in at 6:45 a.m. and the Sergeant greeted me. He took me back to his office, where he told me what was going to happen.

I was directed to follow them to Flint, and wait until they secured the house. They had to be sure it was safe for me to enter. I was the fifth car in a six vehicle procession of unmarked police cars. I followed them into the parking lot of the Jehovah Witness building in Flint, where we were met by policemen in marked police cars from Genesee County. Two SWAT vans also drove up, after a few minutes. I had no clue why we were there, and I saw everyone get out of their vehicles. One of the men came over to my van and had me roll down my window. I saw everyone putting on bullet proof vests. He told me to wait until they were ready. I was wondering where my vest was!

I was told to stay behind all their vehicles and to wait down the block until I received the all clear signal from them. We were two blocks away from the house, which is why they decided to rendezvous in that parking lot. The excitement was building as we drove there, as I had no idea what we would find. My excitement turned to anger when we turned the corner and I saw a van in the driveway of the suspect's house. The photo of the man with Wookie was blown up on each side of the van.

I waited three houses away and saw everyone get out of their vehicles and draw their weapons. They surrounded the house. Two of them brought a battering ram out of the SWAT van. They had it on the front porch, ready to use, and rang the doorbell. I watched as a man opened the door. The police talked to him for a second before having him turn around to be handcuffed. They stormed into the house, and I waited with anticipation for about five minutes. Trust me, those five minutes seemed like forever!

An officer came over to my van and told me to pull into the driveway and wait. Another officer got into my van to make sure I didn't do anything stupid, as two men were escorted out of the house and placed in separate police cars. I saw the man from the photo and stared right into his eyes, knowing he had actually been on my property and stole some of my animals. He saw me and immediately looked down with shame. He wouldn't look at me. The Livonia Sergeant came out after a few minutes and remarked that I wouldn't believe what was in this house. He said there were animals in every room, and that he was glad I was there.

I walked into the house, not knowing what to expect. I saw a large cage in the living room housing three fennec foxes. One of them came running up to me. It was Ben! He was so happy to see me, but I noticed his ears had bite marks and blood on them. I would find out later that the other two foxes were a proven breeding pair, and the other male constantly attacked Ben trying to protect his mate. They never should have been in the same cage.

I was so happy to have Ben back. I honestly never thought I would see him again. I then looked around the room and saw a few large aquariums. Some were empty and the others contained saltwater fish. There was an aquarium on the kitchen counter that housed two frilled dragons. One was in decent shape and the other was almost dead. I asked one of the officers if this was all the animals and he told me we were just getting started. He said the whole upstairs level was full of them.

He said the good news was there were a lot of birds and mammals, but the bad news was there were two pit bulls that needed to be moved out of one of the rooms. They wanted me to move them, as they were scared and unequipped. I have no problem restraining exotic animals, but I'm not a huge fan of having to move two nasty pit bulls. I walked up the stairs. There were six doors, all closed. I had five or six police officers behind me, one with his gun drawn, just in case. Boy, did that really make me feel safe!

I carefully opened the door to what looked like their bedroom. I was told no animals were in there. The police needed to search it first. Once they were done, they wanted me to transfer the dogs from the bathroom, where they were locked up, to this room. I looked around the room while they searched it, and there was nothing I could use to help me move the dogs. I came up with, what I thought, was a brilliant plan. I went downstairs, where they had already searched, and took a door off its hinges. I was going to use it as a shield to guide the dogs down the hall. I carried it back upstairs and told them my plan.

Everyone went down the hall, once the room was cleared, and I was left in front of the bathroom door, wondering if my plan would work. If not, then I was about to be attacked by two vicious pit bulls. I heard their growling and large barks. I cracked the door open and saw teeth coming at me! I quickly shut the door and rethought my plan. The policemen were all behind me, not knowing what was going to happen. I told them to be ready, just in case my plan failed. I pushed the bathroom door open, while holding the other door in front of me.

Both dogs came running out of the bathroom. I started pushing them the opposite way down the hall. There was no room for them to get around the door, because it was such a narrow hallway. They had no choice but to retreat and go into the bedroom. Once they were in, I threw my door down as I closed their door in an instant. I had to hang onto the handle because I realized there was no lock on it, and they could get out. I yelled for one of the officers to find some string or rope downstairs, and I held the door closed until I was brought some rope. I had the officers search the bathroom, because they needed to search every room in the house. Once they were done, I had them close the bathroom door. Since both doors swung inward, I decided to tie their doorknobs together, preventing them from being opened. It worked perfectly. I was now able to go into the other three rooms.

The first room I entered looked like some kind of office. There was a small television with an aquarium under it. I found an African pigmy hedgehog hiding in the bedding. To the left was a desk with a computer on it. There was a large shredder next to it. There were a bunch of documents shredded, and a lot more on the desk. They had tried to get rid of evidence when the police rang the bell. The hard drive on the computer had been erased, but the police were able to retrieve files, once they got it to their lab. There was a small wire cage on the floor with a young coatimundi in it. Coatimundis are native to South America, and they look like raccoons with really long noses. This one was in really bad shape; half of her tail was missing.

I was disappointed that nothing else was there, but I noticed a closet door that was closed. I opened it and saw pine shavings on the floor. A brown blur came at me from the top shelf and jumped onto my shoulder before I could move. I felt something wet on my face and realized it was Wookie licking me! I couldn't believe it! I got a little misty-eyed when I realized it was actually him, and one of the detectives said he had never seen anything like that. I pet Wookie for a couple minutes, placed him into a carrier I had brought and proceeded to the room directly across the hall.

I couldn't believe what I saw when I opened the door. The first thing I noticed was that the room was trashed. The second thing I noticed were five rare toucans in wire cages, three Toco toucans and two Kiel toucans. Whoever built these make-shift cages took wooden branches and just poked them right through the drywall. The birds seemed in good shape. I caught each one and put them in individual carriers. I knew these toucans were worth between $10,000 and $20,000 apiece!

There was one door left, so I opened it. There was a long wire dog run with a Bennett's wallaby in it. Yes, OUR Bennett's wallaby! Peek-a-boo saw me and hopped over. I opened the door to her cage, and was so happy to see her, that I didn't notice the Blue and Gold macaw loose on top. I almost lost my ear, but I moved just as it got to my head. I looked around and saw a smaller bird cage with a Congo African Grey parrot inside. This bird seemed friendly and was talking a lot. It was obviously someone's pet. I placed the African Grey inside a pet carrier and put the macaw in the grey's cage to restrain it.

I picked up Peek-a-boo and put her in a carrier and looked around the room. There was another bird cage that housed two doves, another containing a Quaker parrot and still another with a Sun conure. That was it. No more animals. I looked behind the door and became very angry again. These creeps had kept the pouch I had custom-made for Peek-a-boo, and had thrown it on the floor. More proof that they were the ones who came on my property and violated the law.

I was in for another shock when I went downstairs. One of the detectives told me they had located another residence, and that it might also contain animals. I called my wife, while we were waiting for another search warrant, and told her what I had found. She did some searching on the internet and found a pet shop in Livonia that was missing eight birds. I knew the owner, as I had supplied her with reptiles in the past. Her name was Pat, and I called her and asked what had been stolen. She said a Quaker parrot, a Sun conure, a Blue and Gold macaw, and an African Grey, among others. She said the African Grey's name was Herbie. They were boarding him when he was stolen.

The police said it was all right for Pat to drive up to get her birds. I called the owners of Herbie, as I had to make sure it was their bird. I asked them what Herbie could say. I forgot what they told me now, but I repeated it back then, and Herbie responded. They cried and asked if they could get him. I said sure, and they arrived in an hour. I took them upstairs. They cried the minute they saw Herbie. Herbie came out and gave them kisses; they returned the favor. It was heartwarming.

The police also gave me the ok to contact the owners of the Birch Run Zoo, while we were waiting. I called Lynn and told her that we might have some of their animals. Lynn and her husband drove out to identify their fennec foxes. They told me the foxes were a proven breeder pair, which explained why Ben was in such a bad condition. We didn't know where their tortoises were, at the time, nor was there any sign of their wallaby. We would later find out it had died, from the confessions.

We couldn't proceed until the police obtained a search warrant, so I alternated holding Peek-a-boo, Wookie and Ben, while we waited. My wife, in the meantime, did some investigating on her own. She found a lady in Florida, who had six rare toucans stolen a while back. My wife called the phone number for this woman and found out from the lady who answered the phone, that the owner of the toucans had been bed ridden with depression for over two months…ever since her birds were stolen. This woman's name was Helen, and she got on the phone. She cried when my wife told her about the toucans, which she confirmed were her missing birds. Helen said she was missing three Tocos and three Kiels. She stated that one of the Tocos was her baby that she had hand-raised, and it was a real sweetheart. The thieves later confessed that the friendly one had died. My wife told Helen that I would call when I got the birds safely back to our sanctuary.

While discussing her toucans, Helen told my wife how the thefts occurred. She saw an ad online regarded three large African Spurred tortoises for sale. She called and was told they were only $500 each. Helen decided to purchase them for a friend of hers in Arizona, not knowing the reason for the low price. We would later find out that these tortoises had been stolen from the Birch Run Zoo in Michigan, along with two fennec foxes and a wallaby. Helen made the mistake of telling the man on the phone that she raised rare toucans. Josh, or Adam, I don't know which one, told this nice lady that they would save her the shipping charges and drive the tortoises all the way to her in Florida. What nice guys! They delivered the tortoises and, lo and behold, Helen was broken into and her toucans stolen the very next night!

Helen had no idea these two were responsible, and she had no way of knowing the tortoises were stolen. She shipped the tortoises to Arizona, where they remained, until we told Helen who they belonged to. Helen called her friend and had the tortoises flown back to Michigan, where they were reunited with the zoo.

I called Helen and arranged to ship her toucans back to Ocala, Florida. I set them up in cages when I returned to our sanctuary and took care of them until I could get a flight back to her the following week. She offered a reward, stating that these birds were worth over $100,000. I thanked her anyway, but said my reward was getting some of my animals back. She still sent us a donation for our rescue, which was very helpful, but not necessary.

I'm getting ahead of myself. After waiting a few hours, the police said they had the search warrant and we could go. I followed them to an apartment in Mundy Township, about 45 minutes from where we were. I, once again, had to wait in my van until they made sure it was safe for me to enter. This place was in the opposite condition from the last one. This apartment was clean with no mammals or birds. This one had reptiles, amphibians and weapons…lots of weapons.

I needed to enter a bedroom at one point, and noticed handguns, rifles, a shotgun, too many knives to count, and shirukens (Chinese throwing stars) the police had laid out on the bed. The police were thankful I was there, because we encountered some deadly reptiles. Here is a list of what I confiscated: a crocodile skink, fire salamander, rose tarantula, large African lungfish, reticulated python, Chinese centipede (venomous), milk snake, an albino Argentine horned frog, one albino and one normal red ear slider, snapping turtle, an emerald tree boa, two large Burmese pythons, a baby soft-shell turtle and two Western Diamondback rattlesnakes. They were all in one room!

I called my wife and asked her to do some more investigating online. She called back and said that Stinger's Pet Shop had been broken into; a lot of reptiles were taken. The police called Stinger's and the owners left almost immediately to retrieve their critters. I started packing up the other animals, while waiting for the owners of Stinger's to arrive. They showed an hour later and were extremely happy to get some of their animals back. I left that evening and didn't return to our sanctuary until nine o'clock. It was an extremely long and stressful day, but I was overjoyed to have Wookie, Ben and Peek-a-boo back where they belonged. I placed them back in their cages and set up the new animals. After feeding and watering everyone, I looked at them more closely and noticed that Peek-a-boo's mouth was swollen. I took her to a veterinarian who specialized in macropods and he examined her. He said she had some type of infection, and the prognosis wasn't promising. He prescribed two medicines…one was oral and the other was injected. I gave her the medications as prescribed and bought her favorite food. Unfortunately, Peek-a-boo didn't respond to the meds and died less than one week later. I miss her and still think about her often. She was a real sweetheart.

I also had to take the coatimundi to my USDA veterinarian, because of her tail. Dr. Glikis x-rayed her and found several broken bones in her tail. We assume these thieves grabbed her by the tail and swung her into a carrier, when they stole her. That would explain the broken bones. She was probably in so much pain that she constantly bit her tail, causing the wounds and infection. Dr. Glikis had to amputate the majority of this little girl's tail. It was severely infected and would have eventually killed her, had it not been removed. I gave her antibiotics for two weeks. Once she was completely healed, I found her a home at a private zoo.

The police took another person into custody, Adam's wife. She was involved as much as Adam and Josh. All three of them confessed during their separate questionings by the police. It was discovered that they had robbed zoos, private owners and pet shops in many states, from Michigan all the way down to Florida. I was summoned to testify against them, and it brought back all the anger once I saw them in court. None of them would even look at me. No apologies at all. They were all sentenced to serve time in prison. Josh and Adam were even extradited to Florida to serve time there. Julie wasn't with them during those crimes, so she only served time in Michigan.

I hope none of you have ever been robbed. If so, you know what I go through all the time. It's been over three years since the last break in, and I still wake up almost nightly thinking someone is breaking in. I had steel bars installed on all the windows, had extra security locks installed, and even set up an elaborate security surveillance system because of this…and I still don't sleep at night! It's a real shame that some people break the law and endanger others, while not caring about the outcome of their ignorance and greed.

Jessica and Samson 1992

Me and Samson 1995

Me and Boo Boo

Me and Cindy

Me and one of our many binturongs

Diablo

Our Forest cobra

Cowz

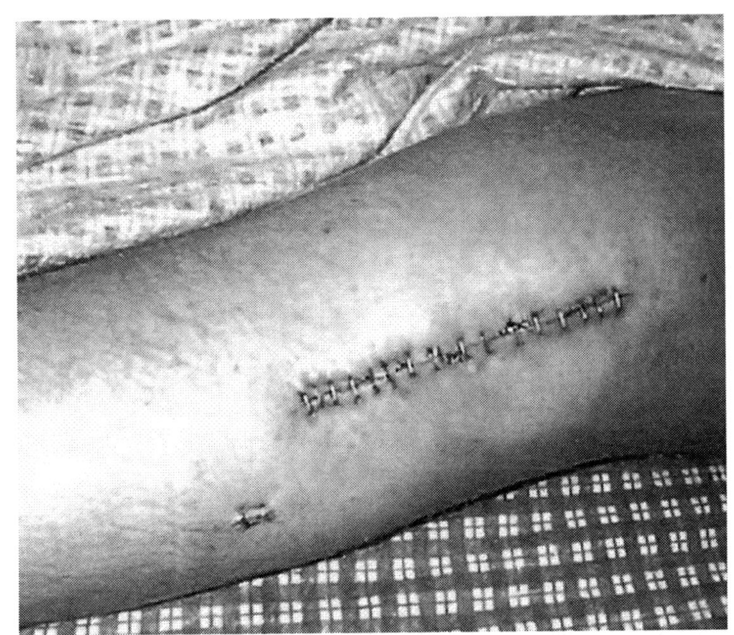

My fractured tibia

Beefy-T-Bad-Boy and another rescue

Professor Einswine

Rickie

My wonderful parents!

Jessica and injured swan

Me bottle feeding Peek-a-boo

Wookie

Chapter sixteen

Hide and Seek

We named another black bear that I raised "Malaika," which is Swahili for "Little Angel."

She was still on the bottle when we obtained her, so we had to keep her in our house. Every baby that I needed to bottle feed was kept on a heating pad on our kitchen counter. I needed to feed them every two hours around the clock. Since the refrigerator and microwave were in our kitchen, it just made it much easier to house them there. Boy, was my wife thrilled about that!

Well, I fed Malaika on this particular day and placed her down on the floor to play while I cleaned her bottle. When I was all done washing it out, I called for her and she didn't appear. She was nowhere to be found. I have no idea how it happened but I ended up losing her. We searched the entire house and couldn't find her anywhere. The more time that went by, the more frantic we became. We couldn't figure out how a bear could just disappear into thin air.

About three hours later, I eventually found her after she had somehow climbed into our dryer, closing the door behind her, and went to sleep. With the sheets or clothes in it (I don't remember which), and I guess they seemed like a nice, soft, cozy bed to a bear cub. I heard her trying to get out when she awoke a few hours later.

Chapter Sixteen

I'll be a Monkey's Uncle

You wouldn't believe how very mean and grumpy an adult, male, patas monkey can be. Especially one I had named Gramps. I don't remember which zoo I got him from, but I do remember that I was in the process of trying to find him a home at another zoo. I could not handle him at all, and he would try to grab anyone who dared get too close to his cage. It was extremely difficult to clean his cage because of his nasty demeanor. We would bribe him with food while we swept his floor and hoped that he didn't attack us. I would throw in some treats and then lean in with a shovel trying to scoot his bedding toward me, so I could bend down and use a dustpan to pick it up.

His cage was six-feet square and made of steel. It was a pretty big cage. Steve was working in the back of our sanctuary one day, a few months after we acquired Gramps and I was up front in my office. I heard a scream and my office door flew open. Steve ran in franticly saying, "Gramps is loose, Gramps is loose!"

After I calmed Steve down and thought for a minute, I figured that I was going to have to shoot Gramps, because he would leave us no choice. I had a dart gun and a 38-caliber handgun as a precaution, just in case anything ever happened. I couldn't risk a dangerous animal escaping through a door or window and hurting somebody. I had no idea what to expect when I opened the door leading to the back of our sanctuary.

I observed Gramps sitting on top of a garbage can staring at me and showing his teeth. Steve shut the steel door, trapping me back there with this loose, nasty monkey. I had to make sure nobody else came in because Gramps would try to rip them apart. A monkey's strength is incredible, as are their nails and canines. He had all of his teeth and he could have done tremendous damage, possibly even killing me. He had the strength of three adult men!

I went to the back of our sanctuary with the gun in my hand not knowing what I was going to do, nor what Gramps was going to do. I had never used a gun before, except at a target range, nor have I ever hurt an animal. I had no clue what was going to happen, but I did know in my mind that if it came down to him or me, I was going to make it. I looked at Gramps and he glared right back at me. Steve was still up front, so I was all alone with Gramps.

I've always been a quick thinker and I still don't know if I was incredibly smart that day or just incredibly lucky. I took a chance and grabbed a banana and coaxed, "Gramps, look." Gramps was so evil that I couldn't even feed him by hand. If I tried to hand him food through his cage bars, he would try to grab me, not the food. Well, I took the banana and threw it into his cage. Gramps looked at me and looked at the banana. He jumped down from the garbage can lid and had a choice of either going for me or going for the banana. He ran into his cage to get the banana and while he sat there eating it, I had time to run over and shut his door. We definitely averted potential disaster that day!

Chapter Seventeen

Walk this Way

My mom became involved with a couple more stories about Samson, one of my African Black-Maned lions. My poor mom. She came over to visit one day when Samson was still a cub on the bottle. He wasn't big yet but wasn't a little tiny baby anymore either. He loved to play. Remember, a lion is a cat…..a really, really big cat!

My mom walked into my house never having seen Samson before. He ran to greet her and grabbed one of her ankles with his massive paws as he accidentally dug his claws into her ankle. We don't believe in declawing or defanging for that matter, so his canines and claws were fully intact.

Picture this…my mom was trying to walk, while dragging this lion across my living room carpet. She yelled to me, "Mark, your lion is attacking my leg. He's got my ankle!"

My response, and I don't remember saying this, but my mom swears that I did was, "Don't hurt Samson. Be careful with him!" I guess I didn't care about my mom; I just didn't want my lion getting injured. What a nice, caring son I am! My mom knows that I love her very, very much.

Chapter Eighteen

Here's Looking at you, Kid

The previous story was my mom's first meeting with Samson and this story was her last. At the time, Samson was three years old and around 650 pounds. It wasn't really fair to keep him any more. I knew he needed more space and room to run. I was willing to give him away to a properly, licensed facility.

The Wisconsin Zoo contacted me saying that they would love to have him. They had a giant enclosure with two adult female Black-Maned lions and no male. Samson would fit right in. I wasn't happy because Samson was a part of my family, but I knew it was the right thing to do for his sake. The day arrived that Samson was going to be leaving us forever. It was a very sad day for my whole family, a day none of us will ever forget.

Samson was my baby and I raised him since he was nine days old. I had spent three years of my life caring for him. I went into his cage every single day to spend some time with him. Not a day went by during our three years together that I didn't go into his cage to play with him. Well, the day came that I was dreading, even though I knew in my heart that it was the right thing to do for him.

It was June 17th, 1996 and it was time for him to go to his new home and meet his new girlfriends. The zoo people drove out to pick him up and they brought a huge cage they had built and loaded into the back of a semi. Samson could sense that something was up and he started pacing. When I opened the door to his cage to coax him out to put him into his cage, he wouldn't cooperate. He wouldn't budge and, believe me, Samson could be extremely stubborn. I decided to take a chance, even though everyone there told me that I was nuts…but you already knew that by reading these other stories, right?

I entered his cage to try to chase him out into the large steel traveling cage. I went into his cage with a big steel barrier that was built especially to protect people who deal with dangerous animals. It has handles in the back, made of solid steel and about four-feet wide by about five-feet tall. Samson was afraid of the steel apparatus and he wanted nothing to do with it. I started yelling and running to try to scare him out of his cage and into the other one. It finally worked after several attempts and he exited his cage into the other cage. I had just scared my baby and I felt horrible, but I knew I was doing the right thing.

Now came the problem that no one had forseen. The steel cage was way too heavy for all of us to lift. We hadn't thought in advance how we would lift a 200-300 pound cage with a 650-pound lion inside of it. We had to lift it about four-feet in the air to get it into the back of their truck. We pondered this for awhile until, luckily, one of the men in a neighboring warehouse had a hi-low and was nice enough to come over offering his assistance. He told me that he never dreamed that he would ever use his machinery to help lift a fully grown lion into a semi in a suburb of Detroit!

Well, we were all crying now, knowing that we had to say our final good-byes to Samson. My parents, daughter and me were all petting Samson and saying our good-byes. It's still hard for me to think about losing Samson, even after 14 years, but it was time for him to leave on his journey to his new home.

I think about him quite often. I even carry around a photo of my daughter and him that's been in my pocket for over 16 years now! One side is Samson as a cub with my two-year old daughter. The other side is Samson as a 650 pound adult with me. It's one of my favorite pictures.

The day after Samson left, my mom had trouble seeing. She went to her doctor and told him what she had done the previous day. After checking her, he determined that she had a very severe eye infection that was most likely caused by lion feces. He probably had some fecal matter on his paws or fur, due to the fact that he was extremely scared when we moved him. It was transferred to her hand while she was petting him and saying good bye. She must have rubbed her eye without thinking and a tiny microscopic piece somehow got in there. The doctor didn't believe my mom at first. She had to show him photos to prove she was petting an adult lion. Her eye was so bad that she couldn't open it. She needed antibiotics for 10 days! There you have it…three stories about my first African Black-Maned lion. I miss you Samson!!

Chapter Nineteen

A Bird in the Hand

I have a Blue Front Amazon parrot named Rickie that I've had longer than any of my other animals. I got her just after she hatched while I attended Michigan State University in 1986. Rickie has been with me every day of my life for the past 24 years.

She loves all men but detests women and children. She is extremely jealous. I raised her at MSU in a house full of guys. There were no kids at college and no women in our house. When one of us had a date, we would leave the house. Rickie was used to males.

My parents came to visit me at college, and we were all sitting at the dining room table playing cards. Rickie was on my shoulder, where she loved to sit. My dad was to my left while my mom was to my right. I wasn't yet aware that Rickie hated women, but I was about to find out, or should I say that my mom was about to find out.

Rickie was talking a lot; she says over 500 words! My mom was loving it. While we were playing cards, Rickie flew over to my mom landing on her shoulder. My mom couldn't believe it! She was so excited, being the animal person she is. She had never had a large bird on her shoulder. This was pretty cool…a large, colorful, talking bird that went out of her way to fly onto my mom's shoulder just to be with her! Rickie sat there for about five seconds and then bit my mom's ear, drawing blood. My mom screamed and reached for her ear: Rickie proceeded to bite her finger. I know it sounds humorous, but trust me, it wasn't funny. I went over and took Rickie away from my mom not knowing at the time what had just happened...it occurred so fast. My mom said, "I didn't know Rickie could fly" and I responded, "Neither did I!" Both of my sisters have been bitten by this bird, as well as my daughter. Countless women have tried to pet Rickie, all to no avail. I don't know what it is about women and children, but Rickie definitely doesn't like either.

She likes to sing opera when I drive. No matter what I put on the radio, I have no choice but to listen to opera. It sounds funny, but it's not, when I have to go on a long drive and all I hear is opera, over and over again.

The good thing is that Rickie will be with me for a very long time. The bad thing is that Rickie will be with me for a very long time. Her life span is 60-80 years and she just turned 24 in August, 2010. She will be with me for the rest of my life and I'll be leaving her to my daughter. Parrots, macaws and cockatoos are not pets for everyone. The lifespan of macaws and cockatoos is 80-100 years! They are very loud and destructive. They will ultimately outlive their owners.

Chapter Twenty

Leaping Lizards

Mongo, who was arguably the largest water monitor in the United States, was from the Toronga Zoo in Australia. He was on exhibit there for years and he was over nine-feet long when I acquired him. He weighed over 100 pounds and was not friendly at all. This was a very large, dangerous lizard.

I didn't have a cage big enough to comfortably house him, so I used a hallway that connected all of the rooms in the front of my sanctuary. This hallway was 20 feet long and about three-feet wide. That was Mongo's home. This was the only place large enough to keep him where he couldn't do any damage to himself.

Monitors are known for rubbing their noses on glass aquariums and in wire cages. This was also the safest place to keep him where he couldn't injure any of us, or so we thought. Mongo was not friendly! We had to be extremely careful when going from one room to another. Even though I loved that lizard, my employees hated him. They were scared to death to have to go in that hallway. We had to carefully walk around or over him when going from room to room. We couldn't disturb him for fear of his wrath.

He was way too heavy to chase anyone, but his tail was his weapon. If he whipped it and connected, it could very easily break our bones. If he missed one of us, then his tail would break right through the paneling on the walls in the hallway and people could hear the noise outside the building…it was that powerful!

There were many times that Mongo would nail me with his tail and there were numerous times that I would time it just right and jump over it, narrowly missing me. Mongo ended up dying of old age many years after I got him. He was one of my favorite lizards and was, by far, the largest lizard I will ever have.

Chapter Twenty-one

I Get the Point!

We rescued an adult female North American porcupine many years ago that we obtained from a private zoo that had no use for her anymore. She was extremely mean and would go out of her way to try and quill anyone who got too close to her. I don't know if you have ever dealt with any porcupines, but they are extremely dangerous. They have thousands of quills.

A popular myth is that they can shoot them, but that is untrue. If they get close enough, they will stick you with their quills and do damage. Porcupines dislodge their quills and each one has a barb on its tip. They enter the skin easily, but they are extremely painful and difficult to remove.

I kept her in a pen in the back of my warehouse until I could locate another facility that could use her. She got out one day. I don't know if one of my employees was careless and left the gate open, or if she somehow popped the latch, but either way, she was loose when I walked back there. She saw me and came charging in full attack mode. This was probably a very humorous sight, because I was running for my life!

Porcupines aren't very big, but their quills are over a foot long. I knew that if she connected with my leg that I wouldn't be able to walk, and I would end up in the emergency room. I was running full speed and she was chasing me, gaining ground with every second. This was an industrial building, so the bathrooms had multiple stalls and urinals. They were pretty big and I ran into one, thinking that I could shut the door and trap myself inside. She would still be loose, but I would temporarily be safe. I would then have some time to decide what to do. However, she was too close to my leg for me to shut the door, so she got inside with me. I was running in this bathroom trying to get away from her and there was not much room to actually run in there.

She ended up cornering me, and had I not been a quick thinker, I would have been quilled. I used cork bark for hiding places in reptile cages. It was lightweight and easily cleanable. There was a piece lying on the floor in the bathroom, about three-feet long by one-foot wide. One must picture this…I bent down, grabbed the cork bark while on the run and swung it sideways from the floor up. It looked like a leg brace-it was directly in front of my left leg, from the knee to my ankle. I used it as a shield and she got me right as I got the bark in place. Hundreds of quills were embedded in the cork bark, but thankfully, none in my leg. She retreated, thinking that she had done the damage. What she didn't know was that she didn't get me, she got the bark.

I ended up getting out of the bathroom and getting her back into her cage without further incident. I still have that piece of cork bark now, over 20 years later, and it still has the quills stuck in it! That's my permanent reminder of what could have been in my leg could had I not reacted as quickly as I did...whew!

Chapter Twenty-two

That's the Breaks

I have many alligator stories and this one had to do with a three-footer named Ally…real original, huh? He was a rescue that we obtained from the Detroit Police Department as a result of a drug raid. Ally was pretty nasty!

I housed him in about one-foot of water in an eight-foot long horse trough. I had a bunch of these horse troughs lined up side by side by side to conserve space. I learned how important it was to never let my guard down, even for a second, when dealing with dangerous animals. Whenever I got hurt, it was my fault…every single time. If I know an animal is potentially dangerous and it attacks me, then I wasn't taking the right precautions…my fault, not the animal's fault.

Well, this was one of those instances where I wasn't thinking. Boy, did I learn my lesson! Among the horse troughs lined up in a row, Ally was in the middle one. There was another trough behind him that had small lizards in it. On that day I had forgotten what they were, reached across the horse trough with my right arm and placed in on the far side of Ally's trough. My arm was extended right over his head. I did this so I could brace myself while I leaned over to see what was in the far trough. Ally flew up out of the water and grabbed my right wrist, clamping down hard enough that he actually fractured my ulna (the bone that makes up my wrist to my elbow). Had I not been thinking quickly, he would have taken off my arm. The surgeons at the hospital couldn't believe that my arm was still attached.

Most of you, if not all of you, have seen or heard of alligators and crocodiles doing a "death roll." Crocodilians don't chew, so they spin or roll, while hanging on until the piece eventually comes off. Well, I'm lucky to have wonderful reflexes. The second Ally jumped up and grabbed my wrist, my left hand instinctively came across my body and grabbed onto Ally's midsection, preventing him from spinning and ripping off my arm. A person can't really pry an alligator's jaws open, so I had to just let him hang on until he decided to let go on his own. If I tried to yank my arm out, then I would have ripped it across his teeth. I was bleeding profusely!

I knew he had done some major damage to my arm. I proceeded to the hospital where I was referred to a surgeon. Dr. Fritz, who had worked on me numerous times, worked me in. She x-rayed it and said that my ulna was fractured and placed my right arm in a cast for eight weeks. The ulna turned out fine, but I had some nerve damage that still bothers me to this day. I also have a semicircular scar of numerous teeth as a permanent reminder of my stupidity.

Chapter Twenty-three

There's No Place Like Home

About 13 years ago, I acquired a giant African Spurred tortoise named Henrietta from a man who had seen one of my performances. He called me up and said that his 11-year-old daughter had raised a tortoise since she hatched from her ping pong ball-sized egg six years earlier. He felt saddened that she was no longer taking care of it the way she needed to, due to school activities and friends. He told me that Henrietta used to follow his daughter down the street like a puppy. He didn't remember why his daughter had named the tortoise Henrietta, but I renamed "her" Henry, after closer inspection.

Non-native tortoises can't live outdoors all year in Michigan because of our cold temperatures. They need 85-90 degrees Fahrenheit all the time; therefore, our tortoises live indoors during the winter. All of our tortoises live in outdoor enclosures during late spring, summer and early fall, since the natural sunlight is highly beneficial to them. We had Henry in a large pen that I built where he could eat the grass outside and also go indoors if he chose. It was great because I didn't have to mow the area where he was or weed it…he ate those too!

Well, we were having a July 4th party for family and friends and we were getting ready the day before. Henry was in his pen. I opened it to feed him and closed the gate behind me, like I did every day. We went to sleep the night before our party and everything was fine. I checked on all the animals every evening to make sure that everything was as it should be.

I awoke the next morning and looked out of my window, because I could see their pens from the bedroom. However, much to my surprise, I saw that Henry was missing. I ran outside and saw that he had burrowed his way under the fence. I thought to myself, "How far could a 70-80 pound tortoise get?" That's what she weighed back then…now she is around 170 pounds!

We searched all over our 10 acres of property and couldn't find him anywhere. I was pretty depressed knowing that he couldn't survive on his own. He could get attacked by wild animals, get run over by a car or get taken by someone who comes across him. I couldn't really go out looking for him since we had about 100 guests coming over, and we had to get ready for them. Once everyone had arrived, I had them fan out and help us look for Henry. We had people everywhere, and there was still no sign of him. We eventually gave up hope. Everyone had either gone swimming, played volleyball or soccer or just sat around and chatted.

Later that afternoon, my phone rang and I picked it up saying hello. A woman's voice on the other end asked me if my name was Mark and if I was missing a turtle. At first, I said no, but then it hit me that she was talking about my tortoise, not a turtle. I asked, "Wait, wait, wait….how big is it?" She said that it was gigantic. She said it just walked right into their backyard. I told her that his name was Henry and that he got out sometime the previous night . I asked her how she knew to call me and she said that everyone knew me around here as the animal guy. She had also seen me numerous times at the Belleville Strawberry Festival and had taken one of my cards. She said that if it wasn't my tortoise that I would probably know whose it could be.

We were extremely lucky that the person who found our tortoise knew who I was and called me. There was a good chance that we would have never seen Henry again. Oh, the kicker to this story is this. Keep in mind that he got out the night before, and it was now about three o'clock the following afternoon. He didn't have that much time to travel and you know how slowly tortoises move, especially one his size. OK, this lady that found Henry lived OVER five-miles away from us! That's amazing on two levels. The first was that Henry traveled over five-miles in a quarter of a day. The second was that he crossed quite a few roads without either getting hit or being seen.

Once I gave her my address, she and her husband somehow loaded Henry into the back of their pickup truck and drove over. I'll never forget the sight of his black pickup truck pulling into our driveway and all of our guests crowding around it to see Henry. My brother-in-law helped me lift him out and place him on the ground, because he was way too heavy to carry all the way to his pen. I started walking back through the gate and onto our property, since we were in front of the house, and Henry followed me like a puppy, all the way to his cage. He walked right on in and proceeded to eat grass just like nothing had happened.

Chapter Twenty-four

Turtle Sunday

Another story involving Henry happened about two years ago on a Sunday afternoon. I constantly pace when on the phone and I was talking to my mom. I was walking back and forth by our sliding glass door in the kitchen when something caught my eyes way back on our property near the woods. We have 10 acres and there is a trail that leads to the back of the property. I'm very observant and I notice the smallest of things. As I was talking on the phone, I glanced outside and said, "Mom, I have to call you back. There is a giant tortoise back in the woods." Then it hit me that it had to be Henry.

Somehow, he escaped again and started to walk down the path. Had I not happened to be on the phone and pacing and looked out at that precise moment, then he would have been gone again! Who knows if we would have ever gotten him back. The trail that goes to the back is only about four-feet wide and he was at the very beginning of the trail. One minute later and he would have been out of sight. I realized that I had to reinforce his cage. I buried a bunch of 4x4s around the inside perimeter of his cage, so he can't dig out again!

Chapter Twenty-five

Be Sure To Use All Your Resources

About five years ago, we rescued a baby black bear that I ended up having to bottle feed. She was young and we decided that it wasn't right to keep a bear in our house. We have our licensed 10-acre sanctuary, but the law states that each bear must have a minimum of one acre. We couldn't justify devoting one-tenth of our property to a bear.

We decided to place an online ad to try to find an appropriate home for her at a zoo or other educational facility. I received a response via email. I asked the man to call me, because I wanted to make sure that he was "legit" and not just some private owner thinking a bear would make a cool pet. He said that he owned a reserve, that he had other bears and that he knew what he was doing. I was wary because he just didn't ask the right questions, in my mind. I had a feeling that I was being set up and I said that to my wife. He didn't ask the following questions that I thought were extremely pertinent to the bear's well being:

1} What formula is she on and how often?

2} How old is she?

3} Does she still need to be stimulated to urinate and defecate or does she go on her own?

We arranged to meet around 1:00 p.m. two days later. My wife, who was my girlfriend at the time, and I were pulling weeds and cleaning up our property in anticipation of our wedding the following weekend. I worried all morning about what would happen if this guy wasn't who he said he was. I decided to take my chances, hoping that it would turn out to be a great home for the bear, which was the most important thing.

A black pickup truck pulled into our driveway right on time and I saw there were two men in the cab. There was a large cage in the bed, and as I walked around to the back, I noticed that it had a government license plate. That pretty much confirmed that I was right and that these guys weren't "legit" bear owners. They got out of the truck and asked to see the bear. They both seemed pleasant at this point so I said, "You're not with a bear preserve, are you?"

The driver said, "No, we're with the Department of Natural Resources."

I responded, "I thought so, because you didn't ask the right questions." I had my wife get the bear and bring it out on the grass. The bear started to play and bounce around; I guess that's all these guys needed to see. They had to make sure I really had the bear before they did anything. The driver immediately became very irate with me. They both pulled out their badges. The driver said that I was in a lot of trouble, and they were confiscating the bear. I told them that they weren't taking the bear anywhere because I knew they were going to put her to sleep. It wasn't the bear's fault that she was a bear! She did nothing wrong and I wasn't trying to sell her or make any money at all. I just wanted to make sure that she was going to an appropriate home.

The driver proceeded to yell, swear and threaten that he was going to handcuff me and take me to jail. I told him to stop yelling and swearing in front of little kids which set him off even more. The other guy tried to calm his partner down (it seemed like good cop, bad cop). It was an awful scene. My wife was outside with our two daughters with one officer extremely irate, threatening me left and right. It's a shame I didn't get any of it on tape.

Eventually the kind officer took over and started talking to me rationally. He said that he knew I wasn't doing anything malicious or purposely trying to make money off this bear. He was nice and asked if he could make a phone call to a licensed bear sanctuary up north, in Oswego. They have over 60 bears and knew what they were doing. I said, "Of course…if you could get him a good home, then that would be great. That's all I wanted in the first place. I didn't want any money at all. That would be perfect."

He made the call and they were receptive to the idea of getting another bear. The officers said they would actually deliver the bear for me, which made me very concerned for her well being. I still thought they were lying to me and would put her to sleep. The nice officer gave me the phone number to the preserve and waited while I talked to the owner to confirm that they were going to deliver her. He said that I could even visit and see her if I was ever in the area. That satisfied me, so I agreed to let them take her.

I picked her up, said good-bye to her and placed her into their cage. I called the sanctuary the next day to make sure she had arrived safely. The owner told me that she was there and everything was fine. Everything worked out in the end, but that was one very rough, stressful day!

Chapter Twenty-six

I Toad You So

My oldest daughter had an unpleasant experience with one of our animals when she was about four years old. At that time, I was one of the largest reptile and amphibian suppliers in the United States, supplying over 1600 pet shops. I had just received a shipment of 1000 Fire-belly toads (which are actually frogs), and I set them up in a bunch of shallow swimming pools with a little water, moss and cork bark.

Fire-belly toads are native to Asia. Their backs are green and black and their bellies are bright red. Just for your knowledge, most animals that have red coloring have it for a reason. It's usually a warning, saying, "Hey, I'm dangerous…stay away from me!" Fire-belly toads have a toxin on their skin. It's not fatal to humans, but it will cause pain and discomfort, especially if one touches them and then eats a sandwich or rubs their eyes without washing the hands real well. They don't bite and they aren't venomous.

Well, my daughter was helping me unpack them and transfer them into the pools. After we were done, I made sure that she washed her hands. She must not have washed them thoroughly though, which I guess was my fault for not supervising her enough. She rubbed her eyes and then started to scream. She was hysterical and complained that she couldn't see. Her eyes were on fire and she was temporarily blinded.

I took her in the house and called 911, who in turn put me through to Poison Control. I couldn't believe what they told me to do! They advised me to take my daughter outside near the hose and to bring another person along to help. They wanted one of us to physically hold each of her eyes open, one at a time, while the other one used the hose to flush them out. Now, to hold down a young girl who was already hysterical, force open her eyes and then run the hose, with that kind of pressure) over them, is insane. There was no way I was going to subject my daughter to those instructions.

She was crying so much that I decided to take her to the hospital, but she fell asleep. That was the best thing that could have happened. When she awoke a few hours later, she was perfectly fine. Her tears had naturally flushed out her eyes. That was the last time I ever let her handle Fire-belly toads or Fire-belly newts, which had the same kind of "poison" on their skin. I learned my lesson the hard way, as did my daughter. Everything worked out fine in the end.

Chapter Twenty-seven

The Jury Is Out

Back in the late 1990s I received a phone call from a man in Nigeria. I was importing a lot of reptiles and mammals at the time, supplying over 1600 pet shops across the United States. This man said his name was Jim Simmons. That wasn't his real name. I changed it mainly to protect my family and me. You will understand why by the time you are done with this chapter.

He told me that he was from Africa and that he was importing reptiles to the U.S. I asked what kind of prices because I dealt with a lot of people. I needed to know if he was in the ballpark or not. His prices were reasonable and I decided to place one order to try him out. I ordered many different types of reptiles and he wanted me to send him money in advance. Now, I guess that makes sense, because why would he send someone he doesn't know animals that weren't paid for? By the same token, why would I send money to someone I don't know in another country before receiving anything?

I decided to trust him and I wired him about $3000. I figured that wasn't a huge amount for an order of reptiles, especially if I was to receive something really unusual. However, I never received anything and I called him numerous times with no response. He finally answered one of my calls and said that he needed more money. He said that something wasn't right with customs. I don't know if I was more stupid or gullible, but I went ahead and wired him more money. I believe it was about $500-$1000. I actually received an airway bill saying that a shipment was en-route to Detroit Metropolitan Airport from Tanzania, Africa. I was very surprised and extremely excited, because there were a lot of wooded crates with my name on them due to arrive the following afternoon.

When I arrived at the airport, I was told that the freight charges were somewhere around $2200. Again, I don't remember the exact amount but whatever it was, I paid it. I didn't know what was in the boxes. When I order from other countries I usually have no idea what they will be sending me. Sometimes they don't speak English and other times they just send whatever they had on hand. I remember specifying that I didn't want anything venomous. Other than that, I had no clue what was in these crates. I opened them up and found some really, really neat reptiles that hadn't ever been imported into the United States. Two species of lizards (agamas) that had never been seen before and an albino Sand boa. Albino boas were virtually unheard of back then, especially one directly from the wild. I was extremely impressed and very happy…so pleased that I decided to place a couple more orders with him.

The next order was a lot of money. I forgot how much, but a lot. The same thing happened again. He called me up and said he needed more money. I forgot to mention that every phone call he placed to me was a collect call from Africa! During one of these calls he mentioned that he was coming here to the United States. He wanted to meet me. I decided to go ahead and meet this guy…that it would be really neat to actually meet my supplier from Africa.

I received a phone call from him on the day he was supposed to arrive. Everything got really weird from here. He said he was at the Detroit Metro Airport and that he needed to get picked up. I said ok, since my sanctuary was only about 10 minutes from the airport. I went there, found him, and brought him back to my facility, because he wanted to check out my operation and see everything.

He was extremely impressed, but he started talking about illegal animals. I cut him off and said that I would never have anything to do with illegal activities. He proceeded to show me diagrams and papers of how he smuggled Pancake tortoises to other people here in the United States. Pancake tortoises are a CITIES I animal, which means they are endangered and illegal to catch, import or export. They got their name because they are completely flat, like pancakes. They max out at a little larger than four inches and they are really neat tortoises native to Africa. He told me, quite proudly I might mention, that he was smuggling them into the United States. He was using false bottoms on his wooded crates and filling the crates with Emperor scorpions. Emperor scorpions are the largest scorpions in the world but completely harmless. He put the Pancake tortoises into the false bottom, which only needed to be about half an inch deep. Picture this: a sheet of wood. Pancake tortoises on top of this flat piece of wood with another flat piece of wood on top of them. The sides were about six inches high and this section was filled with about 100-150 Emperor scorpions.

When customs cracked open the crates to inspect them and saw all of the scorpions, they would immediately reseal the boxes having no reason to look for false bottoms. They didn't want to mess with the scorpions, not knowing if they were deadly. If they happened to remove the whole top and look down into the crate, they would just see a ton of scorpions on top of a piece of wood (the false bottom). They had no idea that there was another bottom one-half inch under that one. That was how he was smuggling tortoises into the country.

I wish he wouldn't have told me any of this in hindsight, because I wanted nothing to do with it. I thanked him for the offer and let him know that I wanted nothing to do with these tortoises. I still have no idea why he told me about this, except he probably wanted me to partake in this illegal act. He then dropped another bombshell on me. He said that he needed money for a hotel. I said that I wasn't giving him money for a hotel and that I just wanted my animals for which I had already paid. He said that he needed money for a hotel. It was always about money with him…more money, more money, more money. Being the sucker I am, I ended up giving him money for a hotel, not a lot, but enough for one night. He wanted $400 or $500 and I think I gave him $40 or $50, at the most. He said he was only staying one night.

He wanted to stay at our house and come back to our sanctuary in the morning, but there was no way I was going to let him see where I lived! I picked him up at the hotel the following morning and drove him back to the airport where he left, and I presumed, headed back to Nigeria. I thought that was weird, that he would come all the way in from Africa for one night.

Well, I ended up getting another shipment from him a couple weeks later. I ordered all kinds of animals and sent him all kinds of money, only to open up the two crates and find toads…hundreds and hundreds of common toads! The boxes were filled with toads and nothing else. I paid thousands of dollars for two crates filled with common toads. That's all he sent. I was shocked. I decided at that moment that I was all done dealing with him. I never heard from him again.

Well, I found out later that he didn't really leave and go back to Nigeria. I never looked at his plane ticket…I had no reason to, nor did I care. It seems he flew to New York to meet with a buyer for the illegal tortoises. After that, I guess he ended up back in Africa.

I received a phone call a few months later from an FBI agent in Chicago. I don't know how they found out, but they had information that I knew how Jim was smuggling the tortoises into the United States. They were going to subpoena me to testify in front of a grand jury in Chicago. They were going to fly me into O'Hare Airport in Chicago with an FBI escort, pick me up and drive me to the courthouse where I would testify in front of a grand jury. I wanted nothing to do with that, especially after they told me Jim's brother was in charge of the Mafia in Nigeria. They had been after him for years. There was no way that I wanted to testify against the Mafia, which would have been suicidal. I said thanks for the call, but I had no idea what they were talking about. I have no idea how they knew, but they said they had proof that I knew. I don't know if my phones were tapped, if they had some kind of surveillance when he was here for that one day, or how, but they knew that I had knowledge about him smuggling the tortoises and how he did it. The agent said that I didn't have a choice.

Two days later, I received a certified letter that contained a round-trip ticket to O'Hare Airport for the following day. When I got off the plane in Chicago, I was met by two ATF (alcohol, tobacco and firearms) agents and a sheriff who escorted me in the sheriff's squad car to the courthouse. We arrived at the courthouse and they brought me through a back door. I was escorted upstairs to an area where there were armed guards everywhere. They told me to have a seat in the hall.

This was not a typical courtroom hearing. I'm pretty sure that none of you reading this have ever testified in front of a grand jury. It was surreal. When

I was called to enter the courtroom, I had to take an oath that everything I was about to testify to would be true and I said yes. There was a judge presiding over everything and it looked like a large classroom. It was pretty casual. It looked like I was in front of a class and everybody was sitting at desks in front of me, even though they weren't desks. They were tables.

I was asked all kinds of questions in detail, dimensions of the boxes, who he talked to while I was with him, who I talked to, what our phone conversations were about, what he shipped me, anything one can think of! I think I testified for over one hour with no breaks. I was as nervous as anyone could be, because I started to think that they were setting me up for something I didn't do. I guess I see too many movies where people get set up for different things and spend the rest of their lives in jail.

I was extremely worried for nothing. Everything was on the up and up and I finished answering all of their questions. I was told in advance that Jim would never know that I was the one who testified. I had to make sure that was clear, because I didn't want my family placed in any danger. I was assured that I would be fully protected. Remember, I never wanted to testify and I never had anything to do with anything illegal. I was forced to testify because this guy from another country decided to tell me things I didn't want to hear.

Well, I got out of the courtroom and I could see they were no longer being nice to me. They had what they wanted. One of the ATF agents sent me down to the lobby with no money and no ride to the airport. He told me that I was to take a taxi and save my receipt to send to the FBI. I took a taxi to the airport and flew back to Detroit. I had no escort this time…I was on my own.

I sent in the receipt and that's the last I heard from them, until about two weeks later. I received a phone call from one of the ATF agents who just wanted to let me know that they told Jim that I was the one who testified. I blew up. I said that I was assured that my name would never be brought up to him and that nothing was ever going to happen to me as a result of this. He said that Jim asked and that they had to tell him. They used me to get this information and then ratted me out to him once they had what they wanted.

This was a long time ago, and I have no idea what kind of prison sentence he received. I know he received some kind of lengthy sentence because the agent told me that they informed Jim while he was in jail and that he had a long sentence. A good friend of mine called me about a year later and said that he had just seen Jim on America's Most Wanted. They showed his photo and said that he had skipped bail and was on the run. I haven't heard his name or heard from him since back in the 1990's. That was my one, and hopefully only, time testifying in front of a grand jury. Not a good feeling, but hey, it makes for a great story!

Chapter Twenty-eight

Ride 'em Cowboy

Here's a quick story about my first pot-belly pig. I didn't know much about them and this happened back when they were "the" craze; everybody wanted one. They are smart, can be litter box trained, and they can live in your house. They were pretty cool and I ended up jumping into the whole pot belly pig craze by purchasing one.

He turned out to be one of the smartest animals I have ever owned. He was so smart that I named him none of the most original names I've ever come up with…"Professor Einswine." He was great. He used his litter box (for the most part) and he loved to open the refrigerator door when I wasn't home.

I didn't know they needed their hooves trimmed, since he wasn't able to file them down naturally outside. I wasn't trained in hoof trimming so I phoned my USDA veterinarian. She told me that she was trained in college but never had a need to actually do it. I made an appointment to see her. I don't know if you know much about pot belly pigs, but they only stay small if you feed them about one cup of food a day. If you feed them more, then they will grow…and grow, and grow. They can attain the size of a full grown pig!

Here's a quick side note on how to tell the difference between a true pot belly pig and a normal farm pig. It's really easy…just look at their tail. The tail of a farm pig is curly, while the tail of a pot belly pig is straight. They actually wag their tail when they are happy or contented, just like a dog.

So Professor was getting pretty darn big. We fed him well and he was probably a little over 100 pounds, when I finally took him to our veterinarian. I put him in a large dog crate. Ok, I attempted to put him in a large dog crate. Boy, was that fun! First, I couldn't get him to go into the crate. Have you ever heard of the term "pig headed?" It couldn't be truer! Pigs are very hard headed and extremely strong. It took forever to wrestle him into the crate, and then he defecated all over it once inside. I finally got it cleaned and lifted it into the van. He broke out before I could even close the van door. He then decided he wasn't done defecating, so he finished all over the back of my van. I cleaned out the crate once again, got him back in, finally making the trip to the vet.

I brought him in and took him into the examining room. Dr. Christine Glikis came in and said, "Ok, can you restrain him while I trim his hooves?" I told her I could try. Well, pigs are nothing like dogs. I worked for Jones Veterinary Hospital for eight years, and I was trained to properly restrain unruly and vicious dogs so neither the vet, nor I, would get hurt. The bigger the dog, the easier it was to get a firm grip on them restraining them. Well, pigs don't have necks like dogs and they are almost impossible to restrain without anesthetizing them. It didn't work out the way we planned.

The vet is a very tiny lady. In fact, Professor Einswine outweighed her! She proceeded to straddle Professor's back and tried to trim his hooves, while I tried to prevent him from moving. Yeah, right! He started to fight and buck, while running right out of the examining room into the hallway. The vet was literally hanging on as if she was riding a broncing bull. It was definitely a sight to behold and one I will never forget. I just asked her about it last week, and she remembered it like it was yesterday.

I don't remember how long it took to finally get his hooves done, but it was hours. Professor Einswine didn't feel anything, it was like cutting our nails or hair. Nails are made of keratin and there was no pain involved, but Professor was scared. This was a brand new experience for him and he didn't like it. Dr. Glikis tried to inject him with sedatives, but it was pretty difficult with a pig. She wasn't sure how much to give and he fought it off pretty well. It never did take effect. She was finally able to get all his hooves trimmed and Professor and I left there a couple hours later. I am so thankful that I never had to go through that again!

Chapter Twenty-nine

The Eensie Weensie Spider

I visited a local pet shop one day after school back in the 70s. It was the coolest pet shop I had ever visited. In fact, I rode my bicycle there almost every day, because they had the most unusual animals. There weren't many reptiles in pet shops 30-40 years ago and Tropical Fish Pond always had a huge selection.

I befriended the owner, whose name was Jeff Gee. He was a really nice guy, and he always took the time to let me behind the scenes to get acquainted with most of the animals. He was very well known and respected in the field of herpetology, the study of reptiles & amphibians. He moved to Arizona and became successful breeding large tortoises. I have no idea how he managed to get in the cage with them! Back then people didn't know as much as they do now about tarantulas.

Jeff had a large Mexican Red Leg tarantula that I loved. I thought it was the neatest animal. She was the size of my hand, and he would let me hold her. I was so impressed that I ended up having to own her. I saved up my money and purchased her without asking my parent's permission. I was probably 13 years old at the time. I brought her home and hid her in my bedroom. I don't remember how long I had her before my parent's found out, but it was quite awhile. After explaining all about her and assuring my parents that she was completely harmless and that she would never escape, they relented and let me keep her.

Here are a couple stories about that tarantula who I affectionately named "Chiller," which was short for "Taranchiller." I know, not one of my most original names, but she did give everybody the chills.

Chiller was really cool. One thing about tarantulas is that many new world ones have little hairs on their abdomen called urticating hairs. Each one has a tiny barb on the end of it, like a fish hook. When the tarantula gets mad or frightened, it kicks its hind legs together really fast, actually flicking these urticating hairs throughout the air at their intended target. The hairs are microscopic so they can't be seen, but boy, can they be felt. They get imbedded into the skin, and because of the barbs, they go deeper and deeper every time you scratch. Believe me…you <u>will</u> scratch because they cause you to itch tremendously. In fact, I read that itching powder is actually tarantula hair! I don't know if that's an urban legend or not but feel free to look it up for yourselves.

Urticating hairs will cause temporary blindness, if they get in your eyes. They will cause your throat to swell, if they land in your mouth. They give the tarantula time to escape from whatever predator happens to be threatening them. Some people are more allergic to these hairs than others. I am extremely allergic to them and some species can cause itching for two or three months! Remember, the more you scratch, the deeper they go into your skin, causing you to itch! I had to explain that, because neither my parents nor I knew about that aspect of tarantulas in the 1970s.

My mom, the prankster that she was, decided to play a joke on my dad one day. He was asleep on his recliner in the living room. My mom had no fear of most of my animals, and she held Chiller occasionally. She was really cool with these animals. She picked up Chiller and placed it on my dad's bare chest. It was summer time and his shirt was off.

Now, my dad was not a huge fan of creepy crawlies and he had never held a tarantula. You have to get a mental picture of this. My dad was lying back with his shirt off and my mom placed Chiller right in the middle of his chest so that the tarantula would be the first thing he saw when he opened his eyes. My dad is one of the toughest men I have ever known and he doesn't show fear…ever…well, almost ever! I wasn't home when my mom did this, or I would have stopped her. Not that I had fear for my dad…I didn't want anything to happen to Chiller!

She placed Chiller on his chest and left it there for him to awaken. My mom said that it was a good thing that none of us kids were home when our dad woke up, because he was using language that we had never heard before! I think he even made up some new words. She ended up having to remove Chiller from his chest, because my dad wouldn't move. I'm glad that he didn't end up swatting her or knocking her off his chest. What a way to wake up from a nap, huh?

Chapter Thirty

What a Swell Mom

Another story pertaining to Chiller didn't have quite as funny or as good of an ending, because it cost me my tarantula. I was at school and my mom decided to be helpful by cleaning out Chiller's cage. She must have startled Chiller as she reached in to clean the cage, because Chiller started rubbing her back legs together, causing her urticating hairs to fly up in the air. Remember, these hairs are microscopic.

My mom had no clue what Chiller was doing with her legs, so she bent down to get a closer look, causing these hairs somehow to enter her mouth. This caused her throat to swell up to the point of her almost not being able to breathe. She ended up having to go to the emergency room, needing different medications prescribed to her.

Chiller was gone when I got home from school. My mom had taken her back to the pet store, because it was too dangerous to have her around the house after what had just happened. It was a good lesson to learn. I now learn as much as I possibly can BEFORE acquiring any new animals.

Chapter Thirty-one

Achy Breaky Heart

I remember the exact moment when I decided I no longer wanted to become a veterinarian. It occurred during one of my Biology labs when I was a junior at Michigan State University. We were learning about how the heart functions and everyone was paired up with a partner. Each team was to pick out a live painted turtle from a bucket that was in the center of the classroom. The professor then demonstrated what we were all to do.

He made a lateral cut from head to tail across the plasteron (the lower shell) and proceeded to remove a section of shell exposing the heart. The turtle was pinned down, so it couldn't move. It wasn't anesthetized. He pointed out how the heart beats and its functions. We were then told to do the same thing with our turtles. I asked the professor what was going to happen to the turtles when we were done with our lab. He said that they would be euthanized.

Well, my partner and I decided that there was no way in the world that we were going to kill this poor turtle that didn't ask for this to happen. We not only liberated our turtle, but we took three other turtles, as well, and placed them in our backpacks. My lab partner and I each took two of them back to our rooms where we set them up in aquariums to live. We received failing grades for that lab assignment and the professor never did figure out where the other turtles went. I hope he isn't reading this book!

Chapter Thirty-two

Girls, Girls, Girls

I lived in a house with two good friends during my junior and senior years in college. The house that we rented was adjacent to a sorority house and right across the street from another one. Is it any wonder that we didn't get much work done?

I obtained a large boa constrictor. My roommates and I set her up in a glass display case in our living room. I built two sliding back doors that locked, since one of my roommate's girlfriends was scared to death of snakes, especially this one, because of its size. I named her (the snake, not the girlfriend!) Jewels, which I thought was an extremely original name. It was short for Julius Squeezer. She was about eight-feet long and extremely friendly. She was a huge hit with all of our friends and we took her out almost every day.

One day, when we returned from class, we noticed that the back of her cage was slid open and Jewels was missing. For those of you who have never owned a snake, let me forewarn you…it will eventually escape; they all do. Well, we searched the house up and down and there was no sign of that snake. How do you lose an eight-foot boa? Sandy, my roommate's girlfriend, wouldn't come over until we found Jules and we searched for her for days, to no avail.

There was a knock on our door a few days later. One of my roommates opened it and came to get me. He said that the police were there for me. I went downstairs to the door and asked what I could do for them. One of the officers told me that I needed to come with them to catch my snake. The police received a 911 call from the sorority next door. It seemed as though Jules somehow got out of the house and climbed into a tree next door. Some of the sorority girls were outside sunbathing and looked up to see a large boa constrictor in the branches right above them. You can imagine their reactions! I don't know how none of us heard them scream but we were told that they all did.

I walked over with the officers and just reached up into the tree and retrieved Jules. The girls came back outside once they saw me holding the snake and eventually overcame their fears after being told that she was pretty much harmless. I even got a date with one of them because of Jewels! I recently got a phone call from Sandy, after losing touch with her over 26 years ago. She reminded me of this story and said that she still has a phobia of snakes.

Chapter Thirty-three

Swan Song

I have rescued three swans in the past couple years and all of them were pretty unusual cases. Two of them involved police calls asking for my assistance. In the spring of 2008, I received a phone call from the Taylor Police Department saying they had received a call about a large swan in the middle of the road. When animal control officers arrived on the scene they found an adult mute swan with the top of its head almost ripped off. It was barely still connected and it was thrashing around in the middle of a major road . They asked if I would come out and help; I immediately drove out there.

I caught the swan and gently placed it into a large crate that I had brought with me. I took it to my USDA veterinarian to see what could be done. She gave me Sulfadine ointment and oral antibiotics for the swan. Our best guess was that it somehow flew into a wire that almost severed off the top of its head. We could lift the flap and literally see inside of her head!

She was pretty listless the first few days, and we weren't even sure if she was going to make it. She eventually started to eat some cracked corn and bread. I knew she was going to be ok, when she started attacking me every time I entered her cage! I had to have my daughter apply the Sulfadine ointment while I held her head still with her beak closed. Their beaks don't really break the skin like a dog's bite but they grab on and twist, which really hurts!

I wasn't sure if she could still fly or if she was brain damaged from the accident, but the day finally came to try and release her. I say "her," but we had no idea if it was a male or a female. We decided to take her to a wetlands preserve about 10 minutes from our house, since we knew there were other swans there. The only problem was, what if she couldn't fly? I was worried that she wouldn't be able to defend herself against predators if she couldn't get off the ground and that we wouldn't be able to get her back if she made it to the lake and got in. I didn't want to leave her there if she could only run and not fly and I knew that she would have the upper hand, so to speak, if she made it into the water.

We drove her to Crosswinds Marsh and noticed other people walking around. I asked them if they could help with her release and they all said that they would love to help. I explained that I wanted everyone to try and block her path to the water once I opened her crate. We would then see if she could fly. If she tried to run, then I was going to chase her and try to catch her while everyone else tried to prevent her from getting into the water. My wife brought the video camera and taped everything.

Once everyone was in position, I opened her crate and stepped back. She wouldn't come out. We waited a little while. I then went back over to the crate and tipped it to try and dump her out. I didn't want to reach in and grab her, causing undo stress. She came out and just stood there. I backed away again and gave her some space. Nothing. We all waited. She just stood there. I took a couple of steps toward her and she started running toward the water. My helpers stood there watching, not really knowing what to do. Finally, she lifted off just as she arrived at my helpers. We all watched her soar into the air. She never looked back. It was a sight that none of us will ever forget. It's truly a remarkable feeling knowing that we saved an animal's life and was then able to release it back where it belonged! I wouldn't trade my job for anything else in the world!

Chapter Thirty-four

Way Down South on the Swanee River

The second swan story happened in March of 2010. I received a phone call from the state police asking if I could come out and help them. It seemed they had an adult swan in the middle of the Southfield freeway blocking traffic. It couldn't fly and it was attacking all the officers on the scene. I said that it would take me about 45 minutes to pack my things and drive there. I proceeded to hurry up and leave.

I jumped into my van and started driving when dispatch called me back. The officer said the swan had just caused a three-car accident and was now on the shoulder. I asked if it had been hit and if I should still drive out there. They didn't really need my help if the swan was now dead. She said that the cars avoided the swan and that's what caused the accident.

I proceeded out there and I saw the accident as I got closer. Then I saw the swan. I called dispatch back and asked how I was to get to the scene, because traffic was now backed up for miles and I couldn't get through. I was given a police escort on the shoulder until I got close to the swan.

As I pulled up, I saw three state police officers on the freeway. One of them had the swan distracted, one had the freeway closed and the third approached my van. She asked if I needed her to call the Humane Society for assistance and I said, "Nope, I'll catch it…piece of cake." I'll let you all in on a little secret. I always say that I can catch any animal with no help, but I usually have no way of knowing how it will go. It almost never goes according to plan. I had absolutely no clue how I was going to catch an irate six-foot tall swan by myself, while running down the freeway with tons of people watching.

I told the one officer to keep the swan distracted while I got my net out of the back of my van. The swan saw me approaching it from behind and started to run down the freeway. I dropped my net and started chasing it. For some reason it couldn't, or wouldn't, fly. You have to picture this sight…the southbound freeway was totally closed, but the northbound traffic was still flowing. I didn't want the swan to jump over the median and get hit or cause a major accident. I knew that I couldn't outrun it. The swan stopped and charged me, probably hoping I would back down. I haven't met an animal yet when I would back down, except for maybe Samson, my 650 pound African Black-Maned lion. The swan realized that I wasn't going to retreat and started to run again. As I gained ground on it, I noticed that I could use the median to my advantage. I got near the swan and tried to pin her against the cement median as we both ran. When I got close enough, I grabbed her neck with my right hand while grabbing both of her legs with my left. I did this while in full stride and it couldn't have worked any better. I caught her in about 10-15 seconds, which was amazing. There was absolutely no way that I would ever do that again. Everyone started clapping! I carried the swan back to my van and put her into a travel crate that I had brought with me. I got it back to our sanctuary and checked it out, but couldn't find anything wrong. There were no signs of broken bones and no external bleeding. I tried to feed it, but it wouldn't touch any food, nor would it drink. It died later that afternoon, but I tried my best to save it. I always feel badly when I don't succeed, but I realize that I can't save every animal I encounter. At least this one didn't die suffering on a freeway or from being hit by a car. My only guess was that it either had internal injuries or some kind of disease.

Chapter Thirty-five

Sitting on the Dock of the Bay

My last swan story occurred in the summer of 2008. I received a call from a lady who lived in a nearby city who knew of me from my Animal Magic shows. She said that she goes to Crosswinds Marsh, a wetlands preserve near us, a few times a week to feed the fish and swans. She saw a swan that had a fish hook in its neck and the fishing line wrapped around its legs, preventing it from flying. She said that her daughter could feed it bread right out of her hand, but she thought it would probably die when the weather got cold because it couldn't fly.

I told her I would come out there and try to help. Again, I had no idea how I was going to catch an adult swan in the middle of a lake, but I would always try. When I got there, I was flagged down by a little old lady who said she was the one who called me. She told me that the swan was in the middle of the lake and her daughter was on one of the docks watching it. I brought along some bread, a pair of needle nose pliers and a knife to cut the fishing line, just in case I could catch the swan.

We walked out onto the dock where we met up with her daughter, who pointed out the swan. I asked if she could get it near the dock. I laid down on the dock and let my left arm dangle into the water. I had her try to lure the swan near my hand with the bread. I knew that I only had one shot. If I failed, the swan would never come near me again. She got it close enough! I swept my left hand up and caught the swan right behind its head. I brought it up on the dock very quickly, because I didn't want to hurt its neck and I didn't want it to hurt itself by flapping its wings. I held it with one hand while I cut the fishing hook in half with my needle-nose pliers. I removed it from the swan's neck with my other hand. I proceeded to cut all the fishing line from around its legs and wing. There was a "ton" of it. There was no way this bird could fly in its condition. Once I was done, I did a quick check to make sure I removed all the wire, and I then released it back into the lake. It swam away and I thought that was the end to a perfect rescue.

But wait, there's more! I went back the following week with my wife and one-year-old son just to see if it was still there. We brought some bread with us and walked out onto one of the docks where there were about 10 people throwing food out to the ducks and swans. There were four swans and a bunch of ducks. None of the birds would come close enough for anyone to hand feed, so we walked out onto the dock. I noticed one of the swans start to swim over to me. I am 100% certain that it was the same swan that I saved. I bent down and proceeded to hand feed the swan that wouldn't go to anyone else. I fed it all of the bread that we brought with us and we left to walk over to one of the other docks where we might have been able to see some fish.

The same swan that ate out of my hand swam over to where we were, and kept following me along the dock. We stayed there for about 20 minutes, and then we walked off the dock. I had my wife and son stay in one spot, because I noticed the swan was still following me. I took a few steps toward the shore and the swan came out of the water and walked right up to me. There were a lot of people watching, as it bent its head down and let me pet it. It wouldn't go near anyone else.

After I pet it a few times, the most amazing thing happened. It started to walk back to the water, when it stopped in its tracks and turned around toward me. It lifted one of its wings, as if to say thanks and good bye, and then it walked back into the water. Other people came over and tried to get it to go near them and to hand feed, it but it stayed in the water where it was safe. We went back to the wetlands a few more times, but there was no sign of the swan. We assumed that it flew back to wherever it came. That was another one of those times when I am so thankful for what I do.

Chapter Thirty-six

Peek-a-Boo, I See You!

Baby kangaroos and wallabies, better known as joeys, stay in our bedroom at night. They are typically kept inside a man made pouch that is hung over the inside of a child's play pen. When they are hungry, or if nature calls, they simply pop out of the pouch and land in the playpen on newspaper that we use as bedding. This approach worked perfectly…most of the time.

One night, as my wife and I enjoyed a peaceful slumber, I was awakened to her screaming, "Ouch." The joey, who we named Peek-a-boo, had jumped out of the playpen, straight over me, and onto my no longer peaceful wife. We put Peek-a-boo into her pouch and went back to sleep. It was my turn to be pounced on about fifteen minutes later. Ok, now it wasn't funny! Peek-a-boo landed on my head and then hopped excitedly around the bed. We turned the light on and looked at the clock…3:18 a.m. I attempted to grab the little bugger and put her back in her pouch, but she had other thoughts. It was playtime now, at least in her mind! Diane and I chased her around the room, but the joey was faster and loved this wonderful new game! Peek-a-boo bounced on each of our three huge dogs, who now thought it was their playtime too. This crazy scene transpired until almost 4:00 a.m., when the little wallaby finally decided playtime was over. She bounced back into her play pen, and right into her pouch, where she fell fast asleep. One's life isn't complete until one has to deal with the crazy stuff we deal with almost every day.

Biography

Mark Allen Rosenthal was born June 4, 1962 in Detroit, Michigan, and spent the majority of his school years in Oak Park, Michigan. He graduated from Michigan State University in 1984 with a Bachelor of Science degree in Biology.

Mark's father introduced him to magic when Mark was eight-years-old. Mark practiced for many years and loving performing for his family. Mark became proficient enough to help pay his way through college. He acquired a job as a magician in 1984 at B'Zar, a very popular nightclub, where he was discovered by a talent agent. He was then hired to perform at the Detroit Tigers 1984 Christmas party, the year they won the World Series.

Mark was asked to perform at a cousin's birthday party in 1980, and he brought along some of his exotic "pets." The rest, as they say, is history!

Mark was hired by Clayton Environmental Research in Novi when he graduated college, and worked there for two years. He then decided to pursue his lifelong dream of working exclusively with animals. He started The Reptile Source, a reptile wholesale company, and quickly became one of the largest reptile dealers in the United States. He supplied over 1600 pet stores in the early 1990s.

Mark decided to stop wholesaling to pet shops and entertain/educate full time when he saw too many stores selling exotic animals to anyone who could afford them, whether or not they knew what they were doing.

This book is for animal lovers everywhere. Come take a journey back throughout Mark's life, as he relates some of his most memorable stories. He promises you will not only laugh, but shed a few tears as well.